KAT

RICI... ⌣

BOOK.

CW00996211

# WHEN IRON GATES YIELD TO FREEDOM

## An Autobiography

by

## MARTIN P A WARD

Ghost Written by Dr Janice S. Lockwood

Grosvenor House
Publishing Limited

The right of Martin Ward to be identified as the author of this
work has been asserted by him in accordance with Section 78
of the Copyright, Designs and Patents Act 1988

The book cover picture is copyright to Martin Ward

This book is published by
Grosvenor House Publishing Ltd
28-30 High Street, Guildford, Surrey, GU1 3EL.
www.grosvenorhousepublishing.co.uk

A CIP record for this book
is available from the British Library

ISBN 978-1-78148-748-8

# CONTENTS

# FOREWORD
## REV. DAVID COLLINSON

I have known ghost writer Dr Janice Lockwood, Martin Ward's close friend and amanuensis for longer than she or I care to remember! She and I have contributed to one another's books, so it gives me a great pleasure to write this foreword to yet another book in which she has been involved. Martin himself I confess I have never met, but I would so love to meet him one day very soon. He is clearly a greatly loved character, whose singing and whose radio broadcasts bring joy and solace to thousands of people.

Not only so, but Martin has a remarkable story to tell, of brutal childhood treatments and sexual abuse at the hands of the so-called "Christian Brothers" at their Industrial School in the suburbs of Dublin; wonderfully loving support came from his brother Paddy, which was crucial in helping him to come through those terrible years, along with his subsequent adventures, linking up with long-lost relatives, and finding a career, a wife and family, along with a place to settle.

The book does, though, leave me with a couple of unanswered questions, one more serious than the other. Why did Martin flee from the possibility of being auditioned as an operatic baritone? More seriously, how did the 'Christian Brothers' come to be the way they were? However did that brutal culture develop? It was reassuring, in a way, that upon release from the Industrial School, Martin spent time in a hostel run by the St. Vincent de Paul Society who turned out to be as caring as the 'Christian Brothers' were brutal. We read of religion at its worse, but we also read of Christianity at its best.

All things considered, the book you now have in your hand is an enthralling story, which, I assure you, dear reader, you will not want to put down. Read on!

Rev. David Collinson
Alnwick
Author of: "Encounter with Darkness".

# FOREWORD
## DR MARK CARRI

An absorbing and fascinating life story about an Irish gentleman who likes to maintain a façade of simplicity to those who make his acquaintance. This book exemplifies to perfection how rich and interesting the lives of seemingly ordinary people can be. His personality springs from the pages and I cannot help hearing his Irish lilt read each paragraph in my head and despite some of the harrowing tales recounted this sound softens the blow as one can sense a profound acceptance and understanding of the time and place in which Martin Ward was born.

# FOREWORD
## DR J S H LOCKWOOD

During Martin Ward's nine long years of confinement in the harsh and abusive Artane Industrial School, it following three formative years in a crummy Dublin orphanage, he possessed no name, only the number of 'Twelve Thousand, Three Hundred and Eighty-Nine', where he obeyed the whistle, where silence became the rule. He has sensitively written, scribing in his imagination, travelling back to his earliest memories and recalling his childhood. As he remained ensconced, fearfully always awaiting unnecessary punishments, sometimes even shocking interrogations, he has re-examined those heart-breaking events which led to his years under the so-called care of the Christian Brothers. At times, when he remembered his late mammy, his absentee father, the memories became almost too distressing as he told the whole truth of his life's story, thus it preserving both his sanity and identity.

At the age of sixteen years, upon his then release from the Artane Industrial School, Martin Ward once again needed to learn to respond to an actual name as given at his infant baptism. Yet, still reliving those dark days of child slavery, of his early years over again and again, there were many occasions when he was actually gripped by a fear, but later more so by the pure joy concerning the beauty of family and friends, with special companionships, taking upon new meaningful relationships, to live once more for the bright every new day. He is obviously aware how everyone suffers, some perhaps more than he; however, whatever hell on earth he went through, he has beautifully emerged now as a truly happy and well-rounded Irish gentleman, full of glorious song, discovering how suffering need never destroy without hope.

This is a gripping adult story which needed to be written. Take heart, dear readers, for whatever shocks you may also suffer, your spirit, like his, can never be crushed.

# ACKNOWLEDGEMENTS

I wish, first and foremost, to thank both the Rev David Collinson and Dr Mark Carri; words cannot express my deep appreciation concerning their writing the forewords. I shall always be grateful for both their scribing. Thank you, gentlemen, for your awesome inputs into my autobiography.

I cannot fail, at this point, to thank Amanda Hobson in helping to complete many of my IT issues. You were brilliant!

Many thanks, too, to Mr Matthew N Bradley for giving up some of his own time and effort in the preparation of this, my autobiography.

My thanks are extended to all those mentioned in the manuscript, who happily permitted their names to be used in the book; some are friends and family whom I love dearly, those who love and respect me.

Last, but not least, I need to thank my very good friend Dr Janice Lockwood for all her kind and various assistance in helping me during the entirety of the book. Without her help, primarily as my ghost writer, neither the first page, nor through to the last, nothing would ever have been reached.

Martin PA Ward
2014

# INTRODUCTION (1)

## WHY THIS BOOK?

"Young people take pride in their strength, but the grey hairs of wisdom are even more beautiful."
— Proverbs 20: 29

Completely enthralled, I sat in my living room, perched on the edge of my sofa, listening attentively to my neighbour. He talking, it was at a highly charged time for him as he'd then become recently widowed. I am truly honoured he has now chosen me to become his friend, to confide in me. Who is this of whom I speak? He is a unique, but quiet gentleman, a softly spoken Irishman known as Mr Martin Patrick Anthony Ward. Martin was genuinely surprised to be called 'unique' for he would modestly state how he is no different to the next guy in the street, but I cannot believe that to be so. I was engrossed as he openly, willingly told me about most of his awesome life, especially his harsh growing up years; through my own previous professional life, I reckon I became emotionally tough, yet, even for the likes of me, it was tear jerking to hear of his formative years in Ireland's abusive Artane Industrial School. Even I acquired a lump in my throat!

Now, personally, I'd only ever been to the beautiful Emerald Isle in the pouring rain. I originally went to visit Alice, another good, long standing buddy of mine. She lives down in Leopardstown, the Irish horse racing venue 8 Km south of Dublin. I began to wonder if it ever stopped raining. Even in the height of summer I rapidly became soaked to the skin! I understand there were a number of industrial schools in Ireland, but Dublin was where the abusive Christian Brothers in the Artane Industrial School were situated. I knew nothing of it then and, while I was in the vicinity, I travelled to visit the famous Trinity College, to view the Book of Kells which is basically a beautifully illuminated manuscript of the four Gospels, in Latin, scribed in 800 AD. Now if that sounds utterly boring to some, I strongly advise you to see it for yourself; it's 100% fascinating. I discovered a little of County Cork, still in the torrential rain. Cork is where, once upon a very long time ago, my Yiddish Granddad met and married a pretty young Jewish lass nicknamed Polly. However, what I was hearing from Martin, now residing in an apartment, in Llandudno's West Shore, North Wales, was way beyond my comprehension.

As we sat in my living room and directly opposite each other, he upon one settee and I on the other, I happened to reminisce, to make some remark concerning the privilege of my own public school days, of the happy times I spent in a Surrey school. Then I was quietened as I heard Martin tell regarding his unnerving early years when he was forced to answer for almost nine years to only a five digit number, as opposed to the registered name of his infant baptism. I can tell you, dear reader, I was shocked to the very core how this now bright and happy fellow should have, in his past, suffered through such dreadful means; yet, as an adult, he has emerged like a butterfly from a chrysalis, as it were, as such a well-rounded, joyful chap, full of a richness in magnificent song. To be saturated in his company is to discover the enigma of a solid life. We are told by some theologians that in Sacred Scripture how the so-called three wise men were so changed by their simply one visit to Bethlehem, that they departed into their own country, yet by another route. I believe it is a little like that for those of us with Martin, for once you meet him, something precious and good will rub off onto you from this incredible guy; after encountering him you'll never be quite the same again. Enjoy and cherish his stupendous Sunday and Tuesday radio programmes, his unique and amazing stories on a Friday afternoon, along with hearing his beautiful baritone singing voice. Hearing him once is never near enough. When my youngest son was small, I used to read him the book: 'This is the house that Jack built'. After I had read it, he would plead for me to read it again and again. It is not unlike the same when I hear Martin sing. One wishes not simply to declare: 'Bravo, Maestro!' but 'Encore! Encore, Martin!' Hearing him once is nowhere near enough and, like the 'House that Jack built', he is in great demand. I personally see him as a legend in his own right. In my humble opinion, for what it is worth, he is always a delight to welcome and hard to leave behind. Only once or twice in a lifetime does one encounter such a great and charismatic man, and Mr Martin Patrick Anthony Ward has to be surely one such a special guy.

As I sat listening to his testimony, he telling of those dreadfully shocking growing up years, first in the crummy Dominick Street orphanage in Dublin, then in the harsh and abusive Artane Industrial School, I recommended he set it down in print, saying of the epic struggles of those gut wrenching years. Oh, he shook his head, trying to shrug me off with one of his broad smiles and a 'What me? You cannot be serious!', yet I was deadly serious; with a dogged determination, I jolly well meant business.

Frowning at him, I stated with almost a plea: 'You dare not allow all those memories to be lost in the mists of time.'

'Whatever do you mean, Janice?'

My own autobiography* was published back in 2008 and I felt his story should also become in a book form. 'Well, all those tales of yours, Martin, your growing up

---

*Janice S Lockwood Ph.D is the author of *'Costly Roots'. an autobiography, written under the pseudonym of Sarah Cohen and published by Crossbridge. Raised in the Jewish sector of Wimbledon, she previously wrote a series of three published books, two booklets (illustrated by Janice Lockwood), her Doctoral theses and a number of commissioned articles, here and in the USA., not least for EWTN's 'The Journey Home'. For her writings a special award was given to her in Florida. Since 2012 until the present she has worked tirelessly as a ghost writer, not least now but as a gift from her to Martin Ward as they scribe : 'When Iron Gates Yield to Freedom'. Widowed since 2008, she had three sons, one of whom is missing following a plane crash; she is now a doting granny to two boys. Until recently, she was an international speaker, many times lecturing in 'writing'. She refuses to accept she is now in her '60's, and resides in a North Wales' resort where she is still trying to understand the meaning of 'retirement'!

Martin P A Ward was born in Dublin, and raised in its Dominic Street Orphanage prior to being subjected to the harsh and abusive regime of the Artane Industrial School. Through 'When Iron Gates Yield to Freedom', Martin Ward has brought sharp and touching hallmarks from the richness of his Irish life; nevertheless, he displays a unique and witty humour, invariably painting pictures through his words. Widower, Martin now resides in a North Wales' town, where, through his love of song and his delight in music, he is a highly popular and successful radio presenter. This book of his is one for you to read and re-read, to meditate upon, to laugh with and enjoy when feeling happy, or leave you lost in tears!

years, your beautiful songs ... as far as possible, write them all down.'

Modest to the last, he simply shook his head. 'Being Irish, I can most probably talk the hind legs of a donkey, telling all sorts of stories, and so on, but, unlike you, my friend, I am definitely no writer.'

'Fair enough, but, only if you're in complete agreement, I could help you by becoming your pen, becoming your ghost writer.'

He continued to think it over, mindlessly stroking his neatly refined white beard. 'All right. I give in!' he exclaimed. He promised to venture wherever his own words may lead and he declared: 'I haven't set things down easily, yet willingly, the words, nay my stories, appear to be now bursting forth from my closet, opening up for all posterity. So, here goes, eh?' Full of encouragements, he embarked upon this his very own incredible journey, to scribe this manuscript through to its completion.'

Before you, dear reader, inwardly digest this book, to settle down for a thoroughly good read, have the box of tissues ready to hand, not only to mop up the welling tears, but sometimes you'll laugh until you cry!

> *Whether the weather be fine,*
> *Or whether the weather be not,*
> *Whether the weather be cold,*
> *Or whether the weather be hot,*
> *We'll weather the weather*
> *Whatever the weather,*
> *Whether we like it or not!*
>
> — *Author unknown*

Janice S. Lockwood

# PROLOGUE

# TO BEGIN WITH ...

I formally made a very long list of many matters about that which I wished to inform you, my nearly running out of paper!

During my recent years, I had composed my autobiography, but only as a journal in my head; now it has emerged like the birth of a new born baby for, after many months, it eventually appeared!

When I stir in the mornings, it is generally somewhat early. When it is needful to surface from my nice warm bed, I seem to lay still, thinking, oh, five more minutes; then I'll get up with a reluctance to face the consciousness of a new dawn. However, when there's no real urgency to place my feet on the floor, I'll swing my legs over the edge of the bed and nip into my kitchen for that early morning's first cup of strong tea, to open wide my curtains, ready for whatever the day heralds, come rain or shine!

Apart from Monday morning's 'Grumpy old Men' and Wednesday's 'talking newspapers for the blind', I know once I am on air, to radio broadcast for four hours on a Sunday, thrice on a Tuesday morning and twice again on a Friday afternoon when it's story time, there shall be faithful listeners to the inimitable strains of my softly spoken Irish voice, to me as a quiet gentleman, with a friendly link into their homes; often those dutiful folk either phone or e-mail, sometimes even waylaying me in the street with requests, with all their immediate musical favourites. Others prefer to hear me sing, truly enjoying the rich tones from a baritone voice. I regularly jest with one particular woman, stating how she's totally biased, my teasing how there'll be no singing on that day from me! Nevertheless, I always simply try to oblige, invariably singing two songs, often from the land of my birth. Not only does she later e-mail her gratitudes, but I have acquired thanks from other regulars, too. One man, I later discovered, stopped dead in his tracks, simply to listen to my singing voice, which inwardly encouraged the likes of me.

Even so, for me personally, there are still the stark shadows of yesteryear, of those wicked men in black cassocks abusing me, stupidly and pointlessly still following me, taking away the Christian name which Annie, my late mother, chose for me and replacing it with the numbers: twelve thousand, three hundred and eighty-nine, to which I mindlessly answered for almost nine long years.

Rudyard Kipling wrote: 'There is a rock to the left and a rock to the right, and low lean thorns between.'

Lord Byron added his own words, penning: 'All was blank, and bleak, and grey; it was not night and it was not day.'

Despite appearing regularly as that accomplished baritone singer, as a keen story teller and a successful radio broadcaster with my own shows, I still seem to hear those abusive men in black from the Artane

Industrial School, echoing around in my head, those who banned me from singing:

> *Somewhere the sun is shining*
> *Somewhere the songbirds dwell,*
> *hush then, my sad reclining,*
> *God lives and all is well.*

> *Somewhere, somewhere;*
> *beautiful isle of somewhere,*
> *Land of the true, where we live anew,*
> *beautiful isle of somewhere.*
>
> — Jessie Brown-Pounds, 1896

However happy and joyful I am nowadays, full of song and laughter, regarding those religious Christian Brothers, it is as if they are still sneering behind me and over my shoulder, always ordering me by that screeching whistle, where silence was the rule, where I dare not either speak or sing in case I received a thrashing.

Nowadays, those now close to me, those precious friends and family who declare they truly love me to bits, will occasionally ask: 'Hello, and how are you, Martin?' Always without either an ounce of bitterness or a false type of self-pity, I reply how I am grand, just grand. Looking around me, it is hard now to see anything but the good, where my apartment gives me a deep satisfaction, where I can put my feet up and do just about as much as I please, where I can sleep in comfort without a screeching whistle, where I can now sing with a happy and joyful way, where no-one tells me: 'Do not sing, do not speak' and where I do not need to 'Run, rabbit, run, run, run,' my racing away across from the years, away from the indescribable horrors of my adolescence. Today, in our twenty-first century everyone is always racing between one place and another in our busy social lives; I believe we need to slow down enough to share even an anecdote, a joke or a reminiscence. We need space enough to enjoy one and another's time. What do you think? Whenever anything came into my head presumably ideal for 'When Iron Gates Yield To Freedom', I quickly had it written down, whether it was an anecdote, a reminiscence, or a story which had a whole lot going for it, particularly concerning our own self image.

Vinny, short for Vincent Ward, our second born son, was probably the happiest of all our children. Raising my two wonderful kids, not least Michelle, Alun and Simon, my three step-children, now all grown up with kids and one granddaughter of their own, I remember only mostly pleasures and happiness – pleasure is supposed to be only for the moment … a sort of a temporary thing. Happiness could well last a whole lifetime. I guess someone remarked, and I cannot, for the life of me remember who, how we should learn to be much more like a happy and joyful Vinny, a then small child, always looking upon the bright side of every human experience. However, to be bereft of parents, as was I and placed into a crummy orphanage prior to the Artane Industrial School, I found, after the midst of a harsh grey winter, as it were, there is dwelling deep within me an invincible summer, but only once I was smelling a freedom well away from the Artane. Herewith is now my own unique story where my life really sparked, where it launched and is constantly sprouting afresh for me.

Martin P A Ward
Llandudno,
North Wales, UK

# CHAPTER ONE

# "MY EARLY YEARS"

'I will arise and go now, and go to Innesfree,
and a small cabin build there, of clay wattles made;
nine bean rows will I have there,
a hive for the honey bee,
and live alone in the bee-loud glade.
And I shall have some peace there ...'
(The Lake Isle of Innesfree.
By William Butler Yates 1865)

Adrenaline surged through my bloodstream like an electric current as I recalled such far gone years when I was approaching four. Invariably, I felt I would rather have locked away those dark and heavy times as I pondered my late mother; oh, she must have so feared that which laymen named 'consumption'. With her sufferings, every endeavour was made by the immediate family to separate me from her; as I was the younger boy, they were frightened witless I might contract her nightmarish cough due to its regular exposure. Thankfully, I remained safe. As she'd spit fresh blood from that wasting pulmonary tuberculosis, she would naturally have feared the relentless pain and the impending doom of death, that dim, lonesome corridor with no choice but to leave me behind, her wee boy; with tear filled eyes, I lost her, too. I missed her more than any of my words may relate to you.

Even now, I am invariably asked by any who possess a deep-rooted care for me, by those who declare their love for me: 'How are you, Martin? How are things with you?'

After a brief and fleeting thought or two, I'll more than likely reply: 'I'm grand,' and again, 'just grand,' instead of verbalizing how dreadfully inept it naturally was; staring straight ahead, rounding a short bend, as it were, I am trying to investigate a fresh those precious and formative periods, so vital in every young child's normal development. For me, though, it's not unlike sweeping away the ashes in the grate, poking finally into the white hot flames and yet preventing a straying piece of coal from spitting out to burn a tiny black hole in the hearth rug.

I'm apprehensive to allow such days entering once more into my soul, my psyche; perhaps using yet another myth, they are more like sharing a bed with a stranger and allowing her to participate in my dreams. Now I am an adult, tall, smart and upright, my sparkling Irish eyes still bright, laughing and greyish-green, my chin strong with a neatly refined white beard; however, then I was a fresh faced, tense, frightened little fellow where, bereft of parents, I seemed to be grasping a single one way ticket to nowhere. I then had no clue concerning those stolen years which have partly vanished into oblivion; it was, maybe, not unlike being in a lift, an elevator and calling in at the wrong floor without any qualified engineer to repair where I was suddenly stranded.

One difficult and memorable day, following my mother's sad death, all the grown-ups in my immediate family, as well as our local parish priest, sat around a dining table; they had all congregated in the Dublin home of one of my aunt's ... well, she was actually an aunty only by marriage, our father's sister-in-law, and a kind widow woman. They'd all met in a unity to work out what should be done with my three sisters, my big brother Paddy and me. Not one of the adults thought to involve any of us children, to speak with us until our futures were a fait accompli.

If my memory serves me right, I think I'd been playing outside in the street, probably mostly with my siblings and cousins with, perhaps, something like either marbles or make believe guns; I was just acquiring the hang of the childish games when I was singled out and brought inside. I was taken to the kitchen's Belfast sink where I was heaved up onto the wooden draining board, soaped and, under running water, had my grubby face and little hands washed. Out of the corner of my eye I caught a brief glimpse of my daddy, but, squeaky clean, I was lifted down and pushed straight across to the big guy in a black suit with a small white collar peeping out; he was the aged parish priest and I was seeing every contour line, all the crow's feet around his bespectacled blue eyes as he smiled down at me. It didn't matter how carefully he put his explanations to me, his soft Irish brogue washed over my young head; the words weren't registering a solitary thing. All I did understand was my mother was in heaven with the angels and I was to live in another home where strangers would care for Paddy and me. I was even more muddled concerning the 'strangers' for hadn't we been told never to go off with them?

I suddenly realized all over again how much I wanted my mother to cuddle me and my grief became chokingly

3

intolerable; why, I wondered, couldn't Our Lady, Queen of angels, tell the ministering spirits to bring her back, fit and well to me? The priest took a clean white hankie from his jacket's pocket, unfolded it and twisted the corner of it to dab my misty eyes, for I wanted to loudly cry, feeling all screwed up inside my abdomen. All I could hear was the priest giving some assurance how our mother was now gloriously happy and free from pain. I wondered how he knew.

Where was our daddy in all this? He mentioned he had heard of a childless couple who would have taken me in, cherishing me as their own child, but, inflexible, he was definite my brother Paddy and I should remain together. Apart from that one and only minor input, he left all the main decisions to the priest, as if the celibate man of the cloth was an expert with grieving youngsters?

I asked if I could remain in the present house with my widowed aunty, with my cousins, but there was literally no room. A smallish terraced house in Crumlin's Downpatrick Road, it was already an overcrowded household with five off spring. 'What if I don't like the new home and the place where I have to live?' I quizzed in between hiccuping sobs. 'What then, Father? Do I have to stay there, eh?'

He hoisted me up and sat me on one of his knees, stroking my pale, tear stained cheek with the back of his chubby fingers. 'You will enjoy it. I promise. Everything shall be simply fine, young Martin; you'll meet other nice wee friends, too. Your brother Paddy will be with you and so you'll be all right. You won't be alone.'

Paddy had previously entered the room, having come in from the Dublin cold; he wasn't too enamoured about the future, yet, seeing me so distraught, he kept quiet in case I became even more panic-stricken. The priest, keen to leave, made the sign of the cross over us all, giving us his priestly blessing of 'Pater et filius et Spiritui Sanctus' before telling me the orphanage would only be a hop, skip and a jump from the Catholic Church. Now, that may well have been splendid in his priestly eyes, but it was certainly no compensation for the likes of me; all I could think about was my mother and I angrily stamped my feet at my terribly unfair loss.

\* \* \*

Much to all my upsets, sleeplessness and against my freewill, along with a whole series of my protestations, I was taken off by the self same parish priest; my brother Paddy, carrying our possessions, naturally came, too. That one momentous Sunday teatime the priest placed us into Dublin's Dominick Street Orphanage. We were only left there because really no-one else, not a single solitary soul within our world was able to take us in, neither a neighbour, nor even a family member. No-one. I believe there was still that couple who were prepared to take simply me, yet excluding all the other four kids, but our daddy refused to have us split up; it was arranged Paddy and I should stick together through thick and thin. Thankfully, as brothers, we were so close, as close as physical circumstances permitted.

I quickly discovered when you're in such a place, you either accept it without questioning and settle down, or you wail from the pit of your innermost being, wishing to God in heaven you were someone else, born into a different era, into a different heritage.

When I had turned four and my brother Paddy was nine, our father was still in the Irish army where, at the commencement of the second World War, he was conscripted. Even though he hadn't volunteered for active service, he seemed to live and breathe the forces; we much later joked how he so loved the Irish army, he was probably marching at the double throughout eternity! It was the army which was paying the monthly fees for Paddy and me to live in the orphanage.

To be utterly frank, daddy wasn't exactly 'father of the year'; I didn't encounter sight nor sound of him until I was twelve, and then only fleetingly. I remember the very day he came. I was out in the playground, staring up at the sky. It was anything but a blue clear sky and it was where the song birds rarely sang, as if they instinctively knew what dark happenings took place to us kids. Although it was part of the summer, there were grey cloud formations, intriguing me how the various shapes became uncertain faces, maybe of people, saints I'd only heard about within the Biblical readings during the obligatory daily Masses. I softly hummed to myself, so quietly even the harsh Christian Brothers couldn't hear my voice: 'I've met some folks who say I'm a dreamer and I've no doubt there's truth in what they say, but sure a body's bound to be a dreamer when all the things he loves are far away.' Someone is close; it couldn't be a Christian Brother or he would have boomed, perhaps giving me either a thump to my ear or a kick to my backside. One of my closest buddies named me 'Wardie' but it wasn't him. Only Paddy referred to me by my first name; fast forwarding some four years, Paddy left the Artane Industrial School, having reached sixteen. Whoever it was, he was not saying 'Martin', but 'Son'. No adult in the harsh Artane Industrial School ever named me 'Son'. I hadn't a clue who he was. Who was this tall upright man, probably in his mid forties, standing by the main gate? The stranger reached out to touch my shoulder and I was permitted to be only briefly led away with him, across the yard, but not into the building, not down the long corridor and up into the chilled dormitory where literally hundreds of beds lined all top to tail. Before him, had he seen it, it would have been the largest of dorms he may ever have viewed. Looking out through the railings, I turned to face him. Once more, he stared through the gradually opening gate separating me from the the outside world and from a freedom. Who the hell was he? I had never received a visitor, not during my time in the orphanage, not at any time in the Artane Industrial School. For eight long years, no-one came anyway near me. Nobody at all.

'I didn't know who you were at first, daddy.'

'Me neither, son. My word, you have really grown. You are quite tall for your age.'

I wondered what he'd expected. The last time he saw me was when after mother died. Did he expect me to have remained a wee shrimp, like a Tom Thumb?

I sometimes would sit on the edge of my bed, my white 'prison', when I remembered I sat with a priest who told me I was going into an orphanage. Now I am in the Artane Industrial School where I am sore in various places from beatings, my neck and shoulders still aching from bending over a stool because of the physical and sexual abuse given to me. I desperately needed that man, my daddy, to provide that which I so craved. I longed for more than affection; I wanted a deep, fatherly love.

During that one and only visit, while we were in the outdoors, some other kids were inquisitively watching. I covered my large greying-green eyes with my hands to exclude them from watching my one and only visit.

'What's up with them?' daddy asked. 'Nosey parkers!'

'Nothing.' I so wanted to blurt out, to tell my father the whole truth about the cruel and abusive Artane, but he wouldn't have believed me if I dared to explain the indescribable horrors. I was afraid to speak of anything but a low voice in case a Christian Brother heard me.

'Do you eat well?' he asked, simply for something to say.

I shrugged. Couldn't he see how pale and thin I was; was he blind to my physique?

'Are you thirsty? What do you like to drink?'

'Why? Do you have something nice for me?'

He shook his head. 'No. I was only wondering ...'

'Tea. We boys only ever get sweetened strong tea. It's that or nothing.'

For some strange reason, perhaps stuck for words, he hummed the old war song of 'Pack up your troubles in your old kit bag' and adding 'Tipperary' to his repertoire. He stared back at the boys as now a group were watching us; he remarked how they were a nosey bunch.

'Shush,' I corrected.'They are my pals and they can hear you.'

Dad began to speak of his time in military uniform, yet I cared not of his wartime fragments. He was sighing, now looking at his wrist watch. 'Well, I have to go now, son.' Before I knew it, he was leaving me back into the hands of the terrible Christian Brothers, my abusive guards and for another four long years.

It puzzled me why he called in on me; as he left, I remember his feet thump, thump, thumping as if he was marching to an accurate count, as if he had his own rhythm. How long could I survive? I considered the question, but if I kept mentally healthy, which I did, well,

I suppose I could survive anything. I lay on my bed and returned to being Twelve thousand, three hundred and eighty-nine under the sharp eyes of the sadistic Christian Brothers.

My dad did bring me a white paper bag in which there were some pear drops, a type of boiled sweet, something to suck, something to share with a few of my buddies; above all, I was left back into myself where only my imagination could run free, to remain brave. He'd only very briefly visited because Paddy demanded it of him, he giving him some cash for his expenses. Never did any of us kids ever hear from him at Christmas, our birthdays, nothing special. Nothing.

I couldn't understand why, in the orphanage, we were in one of the crummiest areas of Dublin. The constant stench from the nearby pork sausage factory wafted our way. If we inadvertently left an open window, I was told it was a worse smell than a horse's backside, although who goes around sniffing at such rears? I know not! The factory would turn on their lights around four – before the light of day and, with my young imagination running riot, I was convinced it wasn't managed by your average Joe Bloggs, but a weird ghostly being! For me, it was simply one scary thing come to haunt me.

As soon as I was somewhat more settled in the orphanage, I was introduced to my first day at the nearby infants' school. Paddy was already a big school boy and was happily settled with the Juniors', but, for me, I had yet to encounter this as something new within my days. I didn't have a parent to take me by the hand and get me to know the kindergarten teacher; to declare upon my second day: 'Oh, no, I'm not going again, for

I went yesterday!' A good half of us thirty orphans were infants, so I simply tagged along and became a school boy, happy to be learning through play, singing and stories. When we infants had painted something really special, the locals would take their 'masterpieces' home, much to the delights of their parents and grandparents. There was no point in my bringing any of my work away, for there was no-one to admire mine; any end of term work, fine as mine was with a succession of gold stars, found its way into the garbage. Nobody cared. When it was sports' day, no-one cheered me on; there was no mother and daddy to hug me and rejoice when I came first in the races.

Only very occasionally, the plump and motherly matron of the orphanage arranged for us kids to be taken to the zoo. Oh, how I loved the zoo! I'd jump and laugh out loud when seeing all the monkeys, with all their crazy antics. On the very rare times when we actually did attend, and it really wasn't that often, a local woman who made chocolates for a living, provided all of us with umpteen bits and pieces of milk chocolate, only her rejects. By the time we came to consume it, it had usually half melted. We'd all try and squash it, rolling it into balls, pretending they were the Easter eggs we never received. Our little hands would be mostly brown and, finger by finger, not neglecting our thumbs, we'd suck away the sticky substance. If our mother was alive and fit, she'd have grabbed a moistened flannel and, holding us still, wiped us clean; she hadn't been around since I was four and, oh, how I missed her love and care, more than my words can still tell.

One day, with the wintry sun low in the Dublin sky, a couple of local nuns from the nearby convent visited our orphanage, telling the matron in charge the Bishop was on his way; matron went into a flat spin, to make lavish preparations. I turned to look up at my brother Paddy. 'Do you think he has come to take us to the zoo?' I asked. 'I really love the zoo.'

Paddy shook his head. 'No, stupid. Bishops don't take kids to the zoo; stop fidgeting.'

I shrugged. 'He might. He simply might; he may have also brought us some bars of milk chocolate.'

Under the watchful eyes of the nuns, we were made to file in pairs and wait out in the corridor; we were seated upon a bottle green cracked leather sofa and told to be as quiet as little mice. Paddy asked why. In a low whisper, he was informed the priest had died. Overheard and somewhat astounded, I added: 'God! Him, too?'

That priest we knew, his lifeless head towards the altar, was completely covered by a crisp white sheet, with the exception of his feet; all of us boys were made to lean over to kiss them. Pressing my lips to his cyanosed, hairy toes made me feel sick to my stomach. I covered my lips with my hand and, panting, raced out. As God is my judge, for at least six or seven months, I experienced the most awful night terrors, looking always to Paddy for comfort, to my new friend Johnny for a big hug. Paddy would also cuddle me, rocking me gently until I slept again. Often I would creep across into Paddy's dormitory, only to know he was with me still, to see he hadn't abandoned me, too.

I believed my brother Paddy, Johnny who became a lifelong friend and I would remain together in the orphanage until we were as big as grown-ups, but, so sadly, it was not to be. I cannot speak for Johnny, but, Paddy and I couldn't remain as our father, no longer in the forces, didn't have the army to pay the fees, and he dodged the regular monthly payments; hence, we were again on the move.

I was convinced we were going on an exciting adventure. A young postulate nun was called in to help the matron pack up all our belongings. No-one seemed to be telling us the precise truth which annoyed Paddy and worried both Johnny and me. What on earth was happening to us? Wherever were we all going?

We were eventually being driven south. Before we knew it, we were motoring over a bridge and I caught sight of the River Liffey where there were boats, I believed, as big as that dead priest's feet! A bill board advertised Guinness and so I had a sense we were still in the city of Dublin. A child like voice within my head wanted to cry out: 'Are we nearly there yet?' although I hadn't the foggiest notion where we were going.

'I'm really, really frightened,' I whispered to Paddy. 'In fact, I am more than that; I am quite terrified.'

'Me, too,' interjected Johnny.

I believe Paddy was also scared witless, but he offered nothing much I can remember.

The black car in which we were travelling eventually came to a halt, parking outside a huge, imposing building.

Huddled together half to keep warm and for also a comfort, we were taken into the County Court House and left in a drab, almost sparse room. The postulate nun seemed to be nowhere around; a woman of about thirty-five, which to us, seemed positively ancient, peered over green ornate spectacles, seated us three upon a long wooden bench and told to wait. We were seated not unlike the proverbial three wise monkeys ... see no evil, hear no evil and speak no evil.

'It is so cold in here, despite that fire,' Paddy remarked, a shudder creeping down his back.

I too shivered. 'I'm really cold,' I told him, my teeth chattering.

'Brr, me, too!' exclaimed our friend. 'I think I'll soon freeze to death -.'

Paddy quickly looked around, noticing two rickety old chairs over in the corner of the room. Mustering all his boyish strength, he began to kick, to smash them up before piling them, stick by stick, into the fire. 'That's a whole lot better! Now we'll be warm, eh?'

With my jaw dropping wide open in sudden amazement, I stared first at my brother and then at Johnny. Paddy warned us to the point of death, not to say a say a single word. 'Do you want to see me in a whole heap of trouble?' he asked with a stern look.

We shook our heads in unison, watching the wrecked pieces of furniture rapidly catching alight and blazing away in the grate.

A court official soon entered the room, to see us three perched still on the wooden bench, remaking how we appeared like little angels. He stated: 'It's nice and toasty in here, isn't it?' The fellow planned on staying with us. He briefly looked around for somewhere to sit. 'I swear there were a couple of chairs in here. Ah, well, never mind - someone must have taken them some place or other.'

'What's happening to us?' Paddy questioned. 'We honestly need to know.'

'All I know is that you shall be taken elsewhere.'

'To another orphanage?'

He shrugged.

'I hope it's somewhere nice,' I added. 'Will we get chocolate and be taken to the zoo?'

He offered a sad sort of a smile, as if he himself was near to tears, but he rapidly blinked them away and bent down close towards my face. 'I hope so, little fellow. I honestly and truly do hope so.'

'We'll all be kept together; right?' Paddy continued. 'We don't ever want to be split up.'

'Yes, I don't expect you shall be separated. Don't you go worrying yourself.'

'Grand. So, where do you think we'll go, sir?'

'Ah now, it is entirely up to the Lady magistrate, but probably to the Artane Industrial School.'

'Artane? Yet another school?'

'Aye. You'll all be very well cared for by some splendid Christian Brothers, so you'll be simply fine.'

If he'd known all the facts, oh, if only he had known!

*** *** ***

Beautiful isle of somewhere:
"Somewhere the sun is shining
Somewhere the song birds dwell.
Hush, then, my sad reclining,
God lives and all is well.

Somewhere, somewhere;
beautiful isle of somewhere,
land of the true, where we live anew;
beautiful isle of somewhere."

(Jessie Brown-Pounds 1896)

# CHAPTER TWO

## "TWELVE THOUSAND, THREE HUNDRED AND EIGHTY-NINE."

'And they were bringing even their children to Him so
He would touch them, but when the disciples saw it, they
began rebuking them. But Jesus called for them, saying,
"Permit the children to come to me, and do not hinder
them, for the kingdom of God belongs to such as these."'
(Luke 18: 16).

When all my basic belongings were being packed up
for me, it was to make sure my junior rucksack was
somewhat less bulky, a little lighter, easier for me to
carry. The matron, who was a kind, middle-aged woman,
placed a motherly arm around my young shoulders
and gave me a gentle squeeze to her ample bosom,
she instructing me to keep my possessions with me all
the time.

'You do understand all this, Martin dear, don't you?'
I stated how I thought I did.
'Listen.'
'To what?'
She raised her eyes heavenwards and sighed. 'To me,
sweetheart. Now there's a little something for you to

eat,' she said, wrapping a knitted scarf twice around my neck.

'What, to eat now?'

She smiled and shook her head. 'No. Not now, dear. It's wrapped up in some greaseproof paper and tucked in the side pocket of your bag ... see? It's simply a bit of a snack if you become hungry. All right?'

I was nearly always famished; all us growing boys in the orphanage were constantly ready for something to eat.

Watching one of matron's maids stripping away my bedding, ready for the laundry, I became more than a bit suspicious how I would never be returning to the orphanage – not ever. When I was only four, I lost my conventionally normal home life once my mother left her earthly abode; as far as our daddy was concerned, he was nothing more than an absentee parent.

I originally loathed the idea of being labelled a poor orphan in a crummy children's home; for the previous three years, however, I'd finally settled. Now to where? I was to be uprooted all over again; I inwardly wondered what would happen to my schooling at St Saviour's National School where I was happily learning, singing and listening to imaginary stories. I was reading well for my years and, sometimes either using my fingers or an abacus, my sums always had a pleasing tick by their side.

What will happen to me, I speculated, if the new place won't have me? Then what? I was feeling as if I was floating in a weird state of limbo ... as if I was in a location of 'nowhere much'. I had heard of unwanted kids being dumped in shop doorways. I didn't wish that for me.

Fleetingly, it crossed my young mind how lovely it would be if I was either fostered out or adopted by a nice family, by a couple desperate to have a child, they who'd simply adore me. However, I was once told by one of matron's staff how married couples who were deemed childless, really only desired blonde blue-eyed baby girls, not now a big boy carrying through life a load of psychological baggage. So, it was the end of that then, huh?

When we arrived outside the imposing Victorian building of the Court House in Dublin, the street was almost empty. Only the brave and hearty had huddled up, venturing out in such icy cold weather; I expected some happy kids would be making a snowman, busily finding two black coals for its eyes and a long red carrot for its pointy nose. I wouldn't have minded playing in the snow.

The juvenile court convened at eleven in the morning. Aware of next to nothing much, Paddy, Johnny and I sat together in an anti-room; all we knew was that we had to sit tight and wait for a garda. He'd take us in to see the magistrate. We waited and waited. Time seemed to drag; a watched pot never boils, eh?

A passing barrister in a curled wig and a Geneva gown was collared by Paddy who asked him if he knew anything about our case.

'Sorry, chum,' he offered in an upper-crust voice. 'You'll have to sit tight until someone comes for you.' He then hurried off to another set of chambers, but not before glancing back at me to give me a wink. I felt vulnerable, having been released from the children's home; my brown shoes looked too heavy for my feet, too much for my thin ankles and legs.

My tummy rumbled and I fondly remembered the snack matron provided. I was about to fish the crusty breaded jam filled roll from my bag, when the garda arrived. He was in his Irish police uniform, but he'd removed his helmet.

'Ready?' he asked. He watched us line up with Paddy heading first, me last. 'You'll all go up in the dock, but, remember, none of you lads has done anything wrong. You are all good boys. Okay?'

We nodded in obedience and filed in, following upon the heels of the policeman, not unlike three little ducklings following their mother.

The magistrate smiled at Paddy and Johnny, but she couldn't, for the life in her, see me. 'Officer, where is Martin Ward?' she asked. 'Where is the young boy?'

The policeman spoke up: 'Martin Patrick Anthony Ward is right here, but he is only seven and a half years of age, ma'am; he is too short to see over this witness stand.'

'Do we have a small box, officer? Something he can stand on, for the court would like to see him ...'

A doddery old guy from the court obliged the magistrate's wishes and I was raised up by approximately six inches.

'Good morning. You are Martin Patrick Anthony Ward?' she asked. 'Do you understand who I am?'

'Yes,' I whispered so quietly.

'Oh, you need to speak up so everyone in the court can hear you. Now, tell us all here, are you Martin Patrick Anthony Ward?'

'Yes, I am!' I exclaimed with a shout, causing most of the assembled folk half grin.

'My word, Martin, you look as if you've been in the wars. Whatever happened to your poor head?'

I looked at the garda who nodded at me to answer. 'Well, I fell over,' I told her, bringing up my fingers to the scab.

The magistrate asked the garda if he knew what happened to me; he didn't.

'Shouldn't the boy be checked over?'

Before the garda was able to say another word, I interrupted with a firm no, nearly falling from my box, but my childish words washed over her; she asked if I had only hurt my head. I informed her with a yes. 'But it only hurts now when I turn over on it in bed,' I stated.

The magistrate shook her head and tutted several times. 'I consider he should still see a doctor concerning his head injury ...'

'I don't wanna see a doctor!' I exclaimed. 'I don't like doctors.'

'But, Martin, do you actually know any doctors?'

'Yes, I do and I avoid her as she has icy cold hands; I don't want her touching me - never, ever!'

'This particular lady doctor has obviously caused Martin some stress, so perhaps we'll see how things go for him ...'

The magistrate said no more about my playground accident.

Paddy, Johnny and I were to go to Dublin's Artane Industrial School, so the clerk of the Court was right, after all; we were to have nice Christian Brothers to care for us. All we needed to do was to sit again in the anti-room where the fire was still blazing away since the old chairs became firewood. We seemed to spend that whole morning waiting.

As we bit into our crusty bread rolls, the door was slightly ajar; we could over hear the thirty-something receptionist. She was chatting away on the phone about a previous luncheon date where there'd been a duck casserole, a simple salad with a dressing, exotic fruits and a cheese board. She told whoever it was, how she'd drop in later. 'I'll come in my Ford,' she was heard to say. Her deluxe version of the black Ford Coupe was supposedly a gift from an ex-lover and, damn him, she was jolly well keeping it.

Paddy interrupted her conversation, asking if we could all have drink. 'Breakfast was a long time ago,' he added. 'We're all so thirsty.'

'You'll all be on your way soon,' she told him, not wanting to be overly bothered with the likes of us.

'Right. In the meantime, may we have something, please? We three are very thirsty.'

'Orange juice be all right?'

'It's much too cold for that.'

'Tea then and with sugar?'

Paddy gave a nod, asking for some biscuits, too.

It all came to us upon a silver tray, full of bone china crockery. Compared with her duck casserole, if she saw our usual tucker, she'd probably declare: 'Don't eat that muck!'

Before long, a tall, thin man, clothed in black attire arrived; he looked not unlike that of a priest in his long apparel.

The man in black peered down at us three youngsters, viewing us in turn. His voice was clipped and sharp. 'Come with me.' He didn't ask by saying: 'Hi there, boys, come along with me; my, it's cold, isn't it?' No. He ordered: 'Follow me now. Quickly!' He seemed to be in a dangerous mood.

I quaked, at first, saying nothing; Johnny was as silent as I, but Paddy, five years my senior, kept a firm grip upon my hand. 'Yes, all right, Father. We're coming.'

The fellow turned to inform spokesman Paddy how he was not a priest, but a Christian Brother. He was the infamous Brother Joe. 'Now, get into car and sit onto the back seat. Move, all of you. I haven't all day,' he snapped. 'Hurry up!'

I gulped, whispering to Paddy how I was so scared. 'I don't like him; I don't want to go anywhere with him; he seems like a bad man.'

'Shush! We have absolutely no choice. We have to go with him, little brother.'

It was as if the Christian Brother found a comfort in anger, and, yet, what about the Masses, his prayers and the lighting of the candles? I was appalled! The idea he called himself a 'Christian Brother' was both fantastic and dangerous. How much did civility really matter to him? I was wishing I could stride back in a vigorous manner, yet my head sagged as I realised my dislike, my immediate loathing of this frightening, impatient, remote, but I was under siege by this vulgar man. Why ever had the juvenile court decided we should go with this guy whose every word seemed to be a threat? If we really and truly possessed a free will, was there any sense in asking: 'Why are we here with this man?'

Who compelled this? Who searched the papers and deemed it necessary to send us to the Artane Industrial School? I suggest the magistrate was somehow confused.

The Christian Brother found his car keys and unlocked the vehicle; opening the rear door, he demanded: 'Get in! Go on, get in.'

Snow was swept up into piles on the edge of the pavement which had frozen overnight. The three of us slipped and skidded over the icy mounds, still aiming for the car.

Upon the back seat, I sat between Paddy and my friend Johnny. I nudged Paddy, pointing down to my foot; my shoe lace had come undone.

The man in black called from his driving seat that I should be able to tie up my own laces.

'Martin can't yet tie bows,' Paddy stated, speaking up in my defence. 'He's only seven.'

The Christian Brother didn't welcome confrontations of any kind; he'd not forget the young spokesperson. I was both so cold and frightened that my teeth were chattering, but Paddy didn't seem to care a dot. He took hold of my foot and tied up my laces. 'There, Martin, you won't fall over again now. All right?'

I nodded, although I felt a fear implanted by the infamous Brother Joe, as if we were being punished in some way for the sad loss of our mammy, for our daddy being unable to financially cope. I knew we were going to a new home and I'd been informed of that several times by various grown-ups, but, when you're only seven and a bit, it doesn't always quite sink in. Was I at fault in some way? I didn't know; I was unsure of anything and everything.

We stopped at some traffic lights and I clambered around up onto my knees to look out of the rear window, from whence we'd come. It had started to snow again and I watched the fluttering snow flakes, some like tiny feathers flying up and around in the wintry sky.

'Sit back down!' the Christian Brother boomed so loudly, that, startled, I swung around and sat down with a flop, snuggling back against my big brother's chest.

Phew, I thought, no-one has ever yelled at me like that before ... not ever. So, why now?

'Are we nearly there yet?' I asked, although I still was unsure as to where.

Paddy knew no more than I, but, to me, he was more than my big brother; he was almost like a substitute father and I loved him to bits. He adored me, too.

'Shut up,' demanded the Christian Brother. 'Shut up, the lot of you. Right?'

Johnny hadn't uttered a single word! How could he be told to be quiet when he had already remained silent?

We three sat in a grim silence; I dared not utter anything more. We obeyed, frightened to almost take a breath more than the normal twenty times every minute.

Arriving at our destination, we stopped outside two enormous wrought iron gates. They were the biggest gates I had ever seen, yet, when your only seven and a half, when you're only a little guy, everything seems thirty feet higher, certainly taller than you. Brother Joe several times blasted the car's horn before constantly keeping his fist on it. Nothing. He sighed, raised his eyes heavenwards and jumped out, ordering us to remain put. He twice rang a large door bell affixed to the side of the gate, and a Mr O'Brian emerged to open up the gates which led us straight into the harsh and abusive Artane Industrial School, under the care of Religious Christian Brothers, where we'd be forced to remain until our sixteenth birthdays.

Eventually, having been ordered out and away from the vehicle, we three, with Paddy in the middle and gripping our hands, we followed the Christian Brother along the length of the snow covered avenue which, to my wee little legs, seemed to stretch on forever; in actual

WHEN IRON GATES YIELD TO FREEDOM

fact, it was no more than a third of a mile. We stopped outside what I later discovered was the monastery building.

I thought about unbuttoning my coat, but, inside the building, it felt almost as icy cold as where the north wind was whipping up and doing its very worse. I could see my breath when I spoke, as if smoke was emerging from my mouth.

The Brother Superior came from the monastery, a building set amidst a five hundred acre farm producing potatoes and a variety of root vegetables. I was soon to discover how the children were their farm workers and wage free slaves. While under the care of the religious Brothers, no boy received even a single penny but only physical and sexual abuse. Not one Brother was ever prosecuted as a criminal by the Irish courts.

'What's your name, boy?' he asked, approaching me first.

'Who, me?' I was a shy child and that was about the best I could utter, failing adequately to reply.

'Well, who do you think I am speaking to? Of course, I am talking to you!'

'His name is Martin, Martin Patrick Anthony Ward,' Paddy spoke up in my place. 'I am his older brother.'

'Shut up, you,' he snapped at Paddy. He turned back to me: 'Now, you tell me your name, boy. So, what is it?'

'Martin, sir. My name is Martin Patrick Anthony Ward,' I replied in my quietest little voice.

He placed his hands on his hips and shook his head. 'Not any longer. You now have a new name. In fact, it is not so much of a name but a number. It is Twelve thousand, three hundred and eighty-nine. So, what's your name now? Tell me, boy.'

'Martin, sir. My name is Martin. That is the name my mammy gave me.'

Swiftly, with a heavy masculine hand, he gave me a smack upon my right ear. He watched me bring my hand up to it. 'Ouch! That really hurt,' I exclaimed. No-one had ever hit me before and my bottom lip was quivering.

'It was meant to hurt. You are not Martin any more. You are now Twelve thousand, three hundred and eighty-nine. So, for the very last time, who are you?' Another thump came on my other ear so hard it knocked me off balance. 'Who are you?' he screamed at me, his reddened face an inch from mine.

I wept and choked out the numbers; tears streamed down my cheeks and I had nothing with which to blow my nose. I pushed my body against Paddy's who asked him to leave me alone; he also just dodged a hiding. Paddy was given a similar number, as was Johnny. Where were we? Hell? Why were we sent to such an institution? I should have to spend almost nine long years until I could inhale the deep breath of freedom, yet much of all which awaited me, what I should experience in the Artane Industrial School was nothing short of a living hell upon earth. I hated it all and there was no means of escape. None.

'Are you three lads hungry?' another Brother came to ask us lads. 'I reckon you surely must now be.'

We each in turn gave him a brief nod.

'All right, then, boys. Come with me.'

We followed him and were led into a dining hall; it was so vast, it could literally house up to a thousand boys. I thought I was going to be be sat down to enjoy a thoroughly good feed, but he offered nothing but bread and dripping; hardly a welcoming treat? I stared down at the ghastly food. To me, with my runaway, childish imagination, it looked not unlike the head of John the Baptist; I wasn't at all tempted to eat it. Was there nothing else on the menu? I wondered. No. There wasn't. I was told I either ate it or I should go hungry.

Well, I thought, I'd rather starve than eat the head of a saint!

'Eat it, Martin,' Paddy told me. 'It's nothing to do with John the Baptist.'

I flatly refused, for I'd have rather eaten cat food.

After I did eventually swallow down the bread smothered in the 'dripping', a fat melted down from roasted meat and used normally for cooking, it was being offered as a cold, greasy spread. Upon the 'doorsteps' of the stale bread, it tasted revolting, but I suppose, if one is hungry enough, then it had to be that or nothing at all.

I hadn't been within the confines of Artane, probably less than an hour or two when three main issues struck me. Firstly, I had lost my Christian name to a wretched number, next I had gulped down dry bread soaked in the unhealthy dripping and, finally, I was amazed by the absolute silence. Considering there were at least a total of nine hundred and sixty boys ensconced in Artane, where were they all? I wondered. It was as if Paddy, Johnny and I were the only three inmates. With no sounds, no school boyish laughter and very definitely no shouting echoing around the corridors, what happened to them all? As we three were taken up the iron steps, walking towards our prospective dormitories, we may well have been in a 'ghost' school, for it was simply as if every child from seven to sixteen years, had got up and left. Even so, we knew this to be an improbability;

I wanted to question, airing my inner known thoughts, yet I was rapidly learning how to keep my mouth firmly shut.

Shivering, I found myself stripped naked, away from my own clothes, such as they were, those I had worn in the Dominick Street Orphanage, they being whisked away, never to be seen again. In their place, I was provided with a two-piece suit of clothes. Apart from the knee length trousers, I appeared not unlike a little old man in my white shirt and the suit woven with its herring-bone zigzag pattern, resembling herring's bones. I held out my arms to receive vests, underpants and knee high socks complete with two elastic garters to hold them up.

I thought that was the lot, but apart from a comb to untangle my hair, I received a tooth brush and a tin of powdered toothpaste. (A friend of mine and a close neighbour recently quizzed me as to what happened when I ran out of toothpaste. Did I receive a fresh supply? Not at all. We were given soot from inside the chimney!)

Standing in my stocking feet, I was fitted with a pair of second-hand boots which pinched and rubbed my feet sore. They were nothing like my exact size.

Not quite seven and a half years of age, I was led into what was known as "Number 5" dormitory, shown to my bed, and promptly instructed how to make it military fashion, complete with hospital corners. The particular dorm was set aside for the youngest kids, anyone below the age of nine years of age.

There was no chance of relaxing upon my bed with a either a comic or a good book; no Christian Brother was kind and every adult was bullying cruel, marching me to wherever. It mattered not, whether it was to meal-times, to the lavatories, to school, or to the chapel for the recitation of the five decades of the Holy Rosary, for the daily Mass or for our slavery work, we marched in step. Out of step and, despite our youth, we were severely beaten.

Night time. After lights out every boy, sleeping in nothing but a cotton night shirt, slept lying flat on their backs; with their arms folded across their chests, they were prevented from touching their own genitalia. A Brother would snooze in an adjoining cubicle, his own small partitioned space, screened for privacy and separate sleeping.

With only the night-light, a dim light kept on all night, one of the young boys would be unwillingly force majeure, a compulsion or coercion to follow the man in the black cassock. Walking behind him, I knew something dreadful was taking place, for the lad always returned to his bed in tears. The Christian Brother, the paedophilia, would choose which boy he desired to rape, for oral sex.

One dreadful night it was my turn. The Brother, having first removed my little nightshirt, tied my wrists up to the head of the of my bed. I was terrified into submission, for he, grasping the top half of a broken hurling stick which possessed a one inch nodule, was shown to me. Hurling is an Irish game, not unlike hockey, yet it is played with broad sticks.

What the hell, I pondered, was that particular Brother likely to do with that frightening weapon? Seeing it, might he beat me? I wanted so much to yell out, to ask him, yet it was as if I was unable to utter a single word; as if all my saliva dried up, my tongue was adhering to the roof of my mouth, stopping my words exiting my lips. I wished to God my brother Paddy was with me, to protect me, but he was far away in another dormitory, prepared for older lads. The Brother constantly observed my reactions as he ran the crazy weapon up along my arm as far as my axillae prior to skimming it along to the soles of my feet, to my inner thighs, closely inspecting my genitalia; reversing the process, he stared into my face, a pale, pinched face demonstrating a deep seated terror. He smacked onto my abdomen. Turning me over, it meant he didn't need to view my frightened, tear stained eyes. That damnable half stick was scratched along the full length of my bonier spine until I felt pressure in and around my anus, causing me to kick and scream, yet silent screams. He ignored my flowing tears as he hurt me, hitting me several times before replacing my nightshirt; hugging me, he nattered on, informing me what might happen to bad boys ... how I should always be good, never telling a single soul what happened.

'You mustn't tell anyone at all,' he declared, showing me a cold bath, complete with a Jeyes Fluid, where I might freeze to death. 'It has to be our little secret. Understand?'

'Okay.' A wee bit of me died that fateful night ... it shall always be dead as I try so hard to bury the memory.

Several times I have since been asked as to what sort of things did we actually do at Christmas when it came to all the nice festive things.

'You mean like a Christmas tree, decorations and the exchanging of gifts?'

'Yes. Exactly.'

'I told my enquirer we received precisely the same as at birthdays.'

29

'Which was what?'

My voice sounded stilted as I informed my naïve friend simply nothing at all. Nothing. It was best I finished the conversation, for there was not a thing helpful to offer. There were few periods of waiting, no real times when I may become excited. From my first beginnings in Artane, to my last, most days were very much the same, day in and day out.

Everything in the Artane Industrial School was by the whistle. Whatever we did, wherever we went, to school lessons, to chapel, the dining room, bedtime, it was by the whistle; silence was the rule - total silence. However, we kids did have times of recreation, play times when my imagination ran riot. We played the same type of games any kid anywhere might play. We'd find a rope and skip for as long as we could. We had spinning tops; we'd twirl them for a while before playing a form of tag, shouting either: 'Ring a levy' or 'Ringolario'. One variation of the game allows the players, in a game of make-believe 'jail', to be freed from the prison, as it were.

During the last Monday in July, on average half the boys who still had families, returned home for a couple of weeks. We orphans who remained, were not unhappy to see them pack up their belongings and go, for it meant acquiring twice our bread ration! The fifty per cent, those of us orphans with no homes, were given a train journey to the sea-side. Always we travelled to Portmarnock, a coastal suburban town in the county of Dublin. We always hoped and prayed for warm sunshine along the fine and wide sandy beach with its five mile long grassy embankments. I was always so excited and loathed waiting, dreading if it rained. God forbid.

We kids were provided with the unusual treat of packs of beef sandwiches one could hardly be regarded as dainty, along with large rounds of teacakes, and all washed down with Cantrell and Cochrell's brown lemonade. I inwardly wished we had some of the chocolate bits and pieces Paddy and I previously consumed when we were residents in the Dominick Street orphanage. It was not to be. I was simply thankful to be a little kid basking at the coastal town, away from the slavery in Artane, only for a day, my splashing in the blue of the sea water; some of the older lads instructed me concerning the rudiments of being able to swim, yet only then with a doggy-paddle style.

With the only wristwatch belonging to one of the Christian Brothers, it showing five O'clock, my mind was full of magic moments, I knew it was time to board the train back to the Artane Industrial School. Prior to leaving the coastal resort, I was able to see out as far as 'Ireland's Eye' where I was utterly convinced there surely had to still be a few pirates lurking. A few boys rapidly mocked me, putting a dampener upon my beautiful day dreams, they saying I was plain stupid. The Christian Brother intervened with his threatening manner, yet nothing, no-one could spoil my day's trip where I savoured every nanosecond, when I was inhaling the fresh sea air with its salty taste, from the seaweed in the water.

During some sunny Saturday afternoons, we kids were often allowed to play out. However, throughout the severe Irish winters, we all sat in rows of wooden seats in Artane's large movie theatre. By the screech from the Brother's whistle every child was marched to view the excitement from the films. It's perhaps my most clear memory, a time when I became inwardly thrilled. I didn't do cartwheels, you understand, yet, for showing those wonderfully watchables, enabled me, simply for that time, to be whisked mentally away from the horrible reality of Artane. Briefly, in my imagination, I was free from the madness of the place, away from those harsh Christian Brothers; I was, in my head, away from my confinement and plunged into a glorious fantasy. I can still rattle off a whole bunch of films, yet one of the now late Bing Crosby's 'The Bells of St Mary's' with its song of the same, is stored forever into my memory, almost as if it's today. I longed to then 'Ooh' and 'Wow' at its viewing, yet I remained under the control of the whistle, where silence was the rule. Whatever, no-one could remove my time from inwardly escaping into another life … another world which bombarded the silver screen.

Sing it with me, if you so wish:

'The bells of St Mary's
Ah, hear they are calling
the young loves, the true loves
who come from the sea;
And so, my beloved,
when red leaves are falling
the love bells shall ring out,
ring out for you and me.'

Within the confines of Artane, we sometimes played football. Irish football differs from the beautiful game played elsewhere. Irish football is a combination of the suspense of soccer, the skills of basketball and the impact of Rugby. Following our matches, I was given the privilege of caring for the balls, my blowing them up and tightening the laces. One of the older lads, yet smaller in stature than I, made some sort of an unhelpful remark, inflaming my fury. It didn't remain with a few harsh words, with name calling. Before the Physical Training Instructor could separate us, we boys were in a fight where I gave my opponent a bloody nose; he was taken off to the infirmary where he was nursed back to health. The PT Instructor informed one of the Christian Brothers who saw it as a menacing means to punish me.

I was made to kneel down and hold out my left hand. Grabbing it by my fingers, with a leather strap, he hit my wrist a full sixty times. If that wasn't quite enough, he repeated it on the other wrist. The pain was so severe, so intense, I fainted. One of my closest friends remained with me until I regained consciousness, he feeling sad for me. He wrapped his arms around me and helped me to my feet, aiding me to the evening school session which began at 4.45 pm. Because of the pain in my wrists, I tended to walk with a heaviness across the floor of the classroom, to which the Christian Brother requested as to why I was slouching, scuffing my feet on the floorboards.

'Come up here, boy. Explain to me why you are making that dreadful noise with your boots.' He took my hands and stared at my blackened, swollen wrists. Knowing he couldn't hit those wrists any more, he made me to remove my shoes and socks. Baring my feet, he promptly hit the soles of my feet, beating first one ten times, then the other to match, before allowing me to sit and read.

At seven o'clock we boys, including me, too, walked across to the chapel to recite the Holy Rosary; the five decades took approximately half an hour. Lining up, we made our way from the chapel across to the refectory. We all had to say grace before meals; as soon as the Christian Brother blew the whistle we could sit to eat. One of the firm rules for eating, during both breakfasts and the supper times was to thinly slice our bread, spreading it with a cheap margarine for breakfast and either the watery jam or the dripping for supper. Because of the shameful condition of my wrists, I couldn't slice my quarter of the loaf, the Christian Brother's eagle eyes rested upon me, he asking why I was consuming the bread in chunks.

'Stand up when I am speaking to you!' he shouted. 'Tell me why you are eating like a pig?'

Nervously, I explained concerning the fight between the boy and myself, about the subsequent beatings upon my wrists, illustrating to him my swollen and blackened condition.

'Get out and face the wall.' The Brother informed another boy he could consume my food, before asking me if I'd seen New York.

I shook my head.

'Ah, now, would you like to see it?'

I offered a nod, declaring how I should one day like to travel.

The evil Brother, not content with allowing me to cope with my present injuries, twisted the sides of my hair, permitting him to acquire a firmer grip, lifting me off my feet, above his head. 'Now can you see New York?'

'No!' I sobbed through my screams.

Raising me higher, the guy asked me a second time, when I yelled: 'Yes, I can see it!' begging, hoping the excruciating torture would end.

'You dirty little liar!' exclaimed the sadistic Brother, allowing me to slip from his grasp, yet not before he slapped me hard across both ears, causing me to feel as if both my eardrums might burst.

All I can remember was suffering intense bodily pain, no, it was more than pain. It was sheer unadulterated agony which no young human should have to tolerate. That night I was unable to undress myself, ready for bed. The overseeing Brother relented, allowing me to remain the night in my day clothes. Was he being kind, having seen my physical state? Not at all. He grabbed me, tossing me face down upon the bed, removing my underpants; sitting on my shoulders, he leathered me. Legs akimbo, he beat me upon my rump and along the backs of my thighs.

Leaving me, he declared: 'Now, boy, kneel and say your night prayers.'

No adult cared. No-one bothered about me, a child without parents, an orphan in the Artane Industrial School. Nobody cared enough to even send me to the school nurse. I reckon I was one step away from happiness, to madness in a crazy and wicked world.

I have touched upon the food rations. To clarify and at the risk of a repetition, at eight every evening, day in and day out, we boys in Artane each received a quarter of a loaf of bread, either smothered with hot dripping or watered down jam. On Christmas day we received two sausages. Upon Easter morning every lad had two eggs, perhaps old duck eggs which stank. Easter Monday each inmate had one boiled egg which could be soft boiled. No-one dare spread their egg upon their bread; it was simply not permitted. I know not why. Morning, noon and night, each boy drank only sweetened tea; it was that or nothing!

It did not matter how we felt and, despite our young youth, we literally worked hard and as penniless slaves, whether we were scrubbing floors, weeding before harvesting fruits and vegetables, to name only a few tasks but, although the incessant slavery remained, everything changed for us at the age of fourteen, when not only were we fitted with long trousers, but where we were groomed for a life skill; there were approximately between sixteen and twenty different trades to choose from, mainly depending upon one's IQ. I was particularly good at mathematics, so, for me, I became skilled within the field of joinery. I experienced a tremendous sense of pride as I beautifully crafted household furniture, along with even smart and shiny floors, with the unique aroma of new wood in my nostrils, with the feel of my own set of tools. For the first time ever, the abusive Christian Brothers left us alone, mostly in the care of tradesmen, fellows who came to teach carpentry, to fire me up to learn in the highest possible standard. I could write chapter after chapter regarding such magnificent creations. Even the Brothers' beautiful Christmas crib where crafted statues of the Holy Family were annually displayed, was hand made to last in our joinery workshop. It was a tremendous time of gradually making and learning and I delighted in those particular far off days.

Sometimes, as sign of adolescent insecurity, a frightened boy might wet his bed. Such problems are not deliberate and scolding merely makes the lad worse. It is futile, in fact, positively harmful to treat the boy as bad, for they are no such thing. Instead of helping him overcome this upsetting issue, the lad would first be openly humiliated, being forced to parade up and down the aisles in the bedroom, covered by his wet bed sheet, prior to being immersed into a cold bath, laced with Jeye's fluid. They may even be made to remain in it throughout the night. This could well have provided the youngster with a degree of hypothermia. There was not an ounce of love, not a moment of either sympathy or care – only a harsh, sadistic regime with Victorian punishments; under the so-called 'care' of those Christian Brothers every day, every morning began at 6.20 am sharp when a whistle blew, it screeching in our ears.

'Truly, I say to you, whoever does not receive the kingdom of God like a child will not enter it at all.' (Luke 18: 17)

# CHAPTER THREE

# "NO STARS IN THE SKY"

"Chestnuts roasting on an open fire,
Jack Frost nipping at your nose;
Yuletide carols being sung by a choir
and folks dressed up like Eskimos.
They know that Santa's on his way ...
Everybody knows a turkey and some mistletoe
helps to make the season bright.
Tiny tots, with their eyes all aglow,
will find it hard to sleep tonight."

(Torm & Wells 1946
Recorded by Nat King Cole)

The month of December heralds in as a whole conglomerate of specific ideas to various types of people. Above all, when we think of that twelfth month, the majority of us tend to remember its twenty-fifth.

To an acquaintance who became a close friend of a friend and who now resides in Brisbane, Australia, Christmas has become nothing much more than a 'silly season', for it seems to begin some six months prior to the real feast, it all so commercialised. She says the real meaning has been lost when even little kids know only about Santa Claus and toys, but nothing much more. Is she simply being a grumpy cynic?

For Terry Waite, some of his Christmases were spent blindfolded and in captivity, as a hostage under guard and without his beloved family. Bored beyond reason, he was reminded of a Christmas as a child. His mother was in her element at Christmastime. A box of decorations was produced from the attic; they had the same ornaments for years. She festooned their living room until it resembled a grotto. Her kitchen grew full of pungent smells: mincemeat, Christmas pudding and sage and onion stuffing. She loved cooking, and Christmas provided her with the one time upon which she could be justifiably extravagant. The Christmas cake was virtually solid with fruit and covered with a good half-inch of marzipan. His father always brought home a goose, needing to be plucked. Terry Waite never remembered any of the actual gifts, but the joy of the wrapping papers surrounding the treasures. Once released, what a 'first' Christmas it must have been in 1991, his own household, surrounded by such a huge family welcome after 1,763 days in captivity

Christmas, despite becoming over stuffed with either too much goose or turkey and mulled wine, it can be a harsh time which invariably reminds us of an empty chair, when a dear one is missing. For some, those first few Christmas times without either one's other half or a child, comes as a stark reminder life is somewhat unfair. However, our joy is complete when a new born baby arrives and steals the show, compensating the proud grandparent for any loss.

December doesn't bring any Christmas cheer for the Jewish people; instead, there's a tremendous festival known as Hannukah, which is a 'light over darkness'. Rebecca, a Jewish friend of mine, when young, around seventeen years of age, asked, as a Hannukah gift, to be taught to drive a car and the following true story was told to me in her own humorous words; sit back and be a little amused:

"'My, you and daddy are back sooner than expected,' stated my mother.

'Home?' my dad questioned. 'It's a wonder we're home at all! It is a miracle she and I are still in one piece.'

'Now, now, dear, don't exaggerate.'

'Exaggerate? I am not exaggerating. Do you know, without a word of a lie, she very nearly killed a cyclist? And then, when I shouted to her to mind the bus, you'll never guess in a million years what she came out with …'

His wife shook her head. 'But you are going to tell me, aren't you, Sam?'

'I'll tell you what that daughter of ours said. On my life, she said: "What bus?" What bus indeed! In the name of reason, how can anyone not miss a great big red double-decker London bus, huh? I told Rebecca, a car is as much of a lethal weapon as … as a gun!'

'All daddy did was to shout,' Rebecca protested, adding her two pennyworth. 'I have never been behind a wheel before and all he did was shout! How can I learn to drive, when he is constantly booming Yiddish stuff into my ear, eh?'

Dad was about to defend himself, but it was his wife who interrupted: 'If you weren't so tight fisted, you'd have forked out for her to have professional driving lessons.'

Raising his dark brown eyebrows in surprise, he spluttered: 'Tight fisted? Me? That's the last thing I am in this household! In fact, my middle name should be called Money-bags!'

The following week, it was with dad's cash, mum arranged for Rebecca to have a series of twenty driving lessons.

'Twenty?' mocked her dad. 'She will need more like one hundred and twenty!'

With twenty lessons under her belt, the day of Rebecca's driving test came. Every time she looked into the rear mirror, there was her dad in his car, following on her tail, for he claimed she was in the car wit a strange man!

'That was no stranger; he was the examiner, for goodness sake!'

'Ah, but you passed your test, didn't you?' Beaming, her dad declared: 'I knew you would. Happy Hannukah, Rebecca!'"

For a Christmas in Ireland it lasts from Christmas Eve to the feast of the Epiphany on January 6 ; this is referred to as 'Little Christmas'. Ireland's Christmas is, on the whole, more religious than only a time of fun.

Lighted candles are placed in windows on Christmas eve, as a guide that Joseph and Mary might be looking for shelter. The candles are usually red in colour and decorated with sprigs of prickly holly.

Irish women bake a seed cake for each person in the household; they also make three Christmas puddings – one for each day of the Epiphany ... Christmas, New Year's Day and the Twelfth night.

After the Christmas evening blow out meal, bread and milk is left out simply as a symbol of Irish hospitality.

Upon St. Stephen's Day, the day after Christmas Day, it is nearly as important with a game of football matches going on.

For the kids, the Wren Boys process. This is a really big event as the lads call door to door with a fake wren upon a stick, all singing with violins, accordions and harmonicas; they ask for money for the poor, which is usually them!

Little ones put out sacks instead of hanging up stockings, waiting for their presents. They also leave out a mince pie and a glass of Guinness for Santa Claus!

When I was a very young little fellow, no more than around about four or five years of age and first living in the Dublin's Dominick Street Orphanage for us young boys, I was totally convinced old Santa Claus just might squeeze down the chimney. I wasn't thinking about the industrial chimney belonging to the nearby pork sausage factory which would open up around four in the morning. No way. I was looking up at the main one on the roof where my brother Paddy, my close friend Johnny and twenty-eight others of us resided. How would would old Santa come for I was aware how he was no light weight? However would such a portly old gentleman, already full of too many mince pies and the glass or two of Guinness, squeeze down our sooty old chimney? It was then, to my young mind, it became quite enigmatic as to how he wouldn't become stuck half way up there.

The majority of my grandchildren are now all grown up; however, when they were then little guys, most of them asked me concerning the self same question, as to how the portly Father Christmas could come down their chimneys without getting stuck. As far as they were concerned, when he came down their chimneys, he'd already downed his fill of some festive foods and drink. I'd smile and gather my grandchildren around me. One or two would be hanging around my neck while another would be clambering upon my knee.

'Tell us, Granddad,' one after the other would plead, 'tell us how Santa Claus will get down the chimney for he is so fat?'

I would begin to explain to each of the little ones in our family by using a thick, strong elastic band. I would pull it out as far as it would stretch without it breaking. I should tell them Santa was as wide simply like that.

'So, what's that to do with Santa?' one would always feel the need to ask.

'Ah, well, listen, sweetheart. Santa is simply like that elastic band, really wide.' All of a sudden, I would allow the elastic band to ping back to its original state; I would tell them how, magically, he can stretch out to his full size and, equally strangely, even squeeze through either a keyhole or down a chimney, before returning with a ping to his full adult size! The demonstration with my piece of an elastic band seemed to satisfy their childish curiosity, only for a while.

As a very little kid, my Irish eyes would widen and wait for something, simply anything to come from Santa. Somehow, I was always left with a crashing disappointment deep down in my heart, with constant tears, welling up and streaming along my pale cheeks.

It was hard not to cry, but those sad days, I believed, caused a *star, my very own star to flicker out in the sky. I was convinced kids who don't have a star make the sky darker. I would try so hard to smile, to light up the sky again, looking up constantly for my own personal star.

---

*See: Chapter 14

I'd been told about the brightest star of all ... something, oh, so special and a star which was followed by wise men from the East, bringing the three gifts of gold, frankincense and myrrh. That was the greatest star of all, resting over where the King of the Jews was born in a stable where, amidst lowing cattle and new born lambs, Mary and Joseph cared for him.

Ensconced in the Artane Industrial School, Christmas brought for me, no magical wonderland, no Santa Claus, he overweight, also smelling from Guinness with the promise of a mince pie on the night before. I bit my lip and sucked in a deep breath, exhaling slowly, for there were no Elves to be seen in his grotto, with no bright star upon a well decked tree with its needles dropping to the floor. There was no point in protesting, for it was as if any gifts, any festivities weren't on the agenda ... at least when it came to us kids. There were no whoops of joy at the discovery of a special present as we'd frantically rip away red and green wrappings, casting it aside once we'd discovered our coveted gift under the tall tree. There were no nativities, no rehearsed plays where a youngster tripped over his crepe paper nativity outfits, where, year in, year out there was the same baby Jesus doll in his same straw crib. No colourful paper chains festooned the ceilings. No one pulled Christmas crackers, wore silly paper hats and read out its equally crazy mottos. There were no girls around to kiss under the mistletoe, but then we were too young to kiss; whatever, it would have been lovely just to be kissed by a friend and hugged by a parent – the reason why Paddy and I were in the Artane Industrial School ... our only crime? We were without parents. That was all. Nothing more.

Apart from our receiving our two pork sausages on Christmas morning, December 25 th was no different to any other day in Artane. We were still penniless slaves to the cruel and abusive Christian Brothers, they controlling us by that ear blasting whistle. None of us was happy and joyful, at least among the boys; we were more likely to receive a thick ear, becoming the victim of abuse, yet remaining silent.

I was ten years of age, and it was my third December 25th and without even either a Christmas card from anyone I knew, a glistening tree ornament or a gift. It was just as if we were forgotten by all and sundry, from every member of our family, immediate or distant; it was as if no one cared about us any more. Was there no-one who loved Paddy and me ... nobody at all?

One day, I thought, when I am free from here, from this God forsaken place, when I am all grown up, I'll fill my home with festive stuff; I shall buy an over stuffed turkey with all the trimmings, but, in the meantime, there was nothing but that wretched whistle is blown in my ears by those wicked and sadistic Christian Brothers.

A painted white line in the courtyard divided the older rougher kids from us little ones. We were not allowed to communicate. Paddy, being some years older than I, had done his utmost to care for me, despite that damn whitened line. We'd stand either side of the division with our backs to each other and try to talk, hoping we'd neither be seen nor heard, for it would mean certain punishment from the overly powerful Brother Joe who we boys nicknamed: "Joe-Boy".

My beloved Paddy had somehow acquired a bottle of Cantrell and Cochrane's brown lemonade. I suppose it was a little like our coca cola. Having taken a little sip himself, he passed the remaining beverage to me.

'Happy Christmas, little brother,' he stated in a loud whisper to me.' This is for you, Martin. This is for you for Christmas. Okay?'

'For me?' I questioned. 'For me for Christmas?'

'Shush, Martin. You should know by now to keep your voice down!'

This was my first ever gift, my first Christmas present since I'd come to Artane.

I tried to conceal it, tucking it under my shirt, but the nasty Brother Joe spied the contraband.

'What have you there, Twelve thousand, three hundred and eighty-nine?' he asked. 'Speak up!'

I scowled. 'Nothing ... nothing whatsoever, sir.'

'You bare faced little liar!' With a sense of menace, he punched me hard in my ear, leaving it red and sore. 'Whatever you have, give it to me now, or I shall hit you again!'

I angled my head in defiance and refused, but he yanked my wrist, snatching the torpedo style bottle from my grip. He held it at arm's length, looked at the label, staring back at me with a grin.

'Please, sir, it's for me; it's for Christmas.'

'Is it really? Fancy that!' He pulled out the cork stopper and, constantly watching my reaction, turned the bottle upside down, slowly pouring the lemonade onto the ground, just missing the toes of my black boots; not a single drop remained. He watched me and threw his head back and laughed once he saw the tears running down my cheeks, as I sniffed and wiped them away with the back of my hand.

'Cry baby!' he exclaimed.

'At least let me have the bottle, please?' I choked. I knew I could exchange the empty container for some pennies, money I could use locally to buy sweets.

He refused, kicking it away from my sight, but he accused me of leaving litter behind. 'You bad lad! You know better than to do such a thing, don't you?' So once more he hit me.

Such a gut-wrenching disappointment, it was my first Christmas gift ever, and it was made even more special because it came from my brother Paddy. I was genuinely happy for him as he would soon be free, free from Artane once he reached his sixteenth birthday, then, he stated, he would take crap from no-one.

When my brother Paddy was once and for all about to take his leave from that severe institution, the Christian Brothers refused, for some unknown reason and only known to them, banning us from saying our fond farewells. Paddy and I so much wanted to hug, for me to wish him good luck, to tell each other we loved one another. All our pleadings fell upon deaf ears, for, as far as the Brothers were concerned, that was the end of the matter.

I stood as near as I dare, squinting to see my tall and handsome Paddy; for me, I cupped an ear with my hand, to try to strain to hear his parting words.

Paddy heaved a great breath in and yelled at the top of his voice, cupping both his hands around his mouth: 'See you real soon. Keep safe, Martin! Remember, we are always brothers!'

One of the nastiest of the Christian Brothers poked me hard in between my shoulder blades which hurt like hell upon earth: 'Get yourself back inside or I shall thrash you! Do you want a thrashing? Go on. Answer me!'

'No.'

'What? Speak up, boy! Has the cat got your tongue?'

'No, sir. I don't want any more thrashings!'

47

It takes no time at all to figure out what was wrong, what three things were missing, what lacked from Artane in that beautiful land, that city which is Dublin … love, patience and understanding were omitted from that harsh and abusive industrial school.

\* \* \*

## GOING MY WAY

"In time gone by, I lost my will
to try and find a clear way through;
Now it's been a while
since I asked myself what to do;
it's been a while since I played the fool
'cos they said: 'raise your game, leave
the shame in this place where you will remain
unless you save your soul'.

Now it's going my way
forget the time that I did then
now it's going my way;
I look and everything's okay.
I've nothing much to say except
The life I now lead
is going my way,
going my way!

It's been a while since I spent the day
the whole day wrapped up in my dreams;
it took a while upstaging misery.
It isn't all it seems.
Now I smooth my hair, feeling tight;
I am getting into something right,
living beyond those days."

# CHAPTER FOUR

### "TAKE YOUR BIKE!"

When I was growing up in Dublin's Artane Industrial School, delirious with boredom, there was always a paralysing terror which hung in the air. I winced as the echo of a victim's screams reverberated inside my head. My stomach cramped; disgust and fear emanated from being with those so-called 'Christian' Brothers, from all those formative years under their harsh and abusive regime.

Until that most memorable day, the day of freedom ... my freedom, I believed, ooh, one day folk would raise the standard and simultaneously show me a respect by calling me by my actual names; they'd no longer simply shout out at me by that five digit number of 'Twelve thousand, three hundred and eighty-nine'; not a chance!

It is invariably tough to wait for a highly special event, whatever it may be, but when you're only a young kid longing to leave behind somewhere such as Artane Industrial School, well, it was a whole new ball game. To be frank, I could hardly wait. I shared a few bites of an apple with a close buddy who had a little longer to serve than I.

'I betcha can't wait, eh?' he stated.

Too right; I couldn't hardly wait, yet I should need to remain for another one hundred and fifteen days, yet my apple munching friend had the notion to work it all out in seconds!

'Seconds!' I gasped. 'How many?'

'In nine million, nine hundred and thirty-four thousand seconds, Wardie, you shall be walking free, free as a bird in flight and well away from those rotten Christian Brothers!'

The twenty-third of February finally showed up on the 1955 calendar. I'd eventually reached my sixteenth year and, at eight 0'clock in the morning, fifty-seven thousand, six hundred seconds earlier than my buddy and I had stated, I was about to leave that Artane Industrial School once and for all, to acquire an independence which was constantly beckoning to me. Half closing my grey green eyes, I cherished the word: 'freedom'. I so wanted to raise and wave my arms heavenwards, dance a jig and throw back my head; I actually desired to sing out the word 'freedom' loud and clear, yet I didn't dare while I was still on Artane's soil. Nine years before, as a frightened seven and a bit year old, I swung back to glance at those high wrought iron gates closing me in, to hear them shut with a clunking slam. Now, one of those massive gates would creak its way to open up, allowing me to step out into my new life, beginning with Dublin's fair city, the place of my birth, before heading for a paradise; anywhere would be a glorious haven compared with the years of cruel and abusive incarceration in Artane and yet, as I strutted along the avenue, I was choking back my welling tears; the salty tears then began to stream down the pallor of my cheeks. For all its gross badness, for all its unnecessary cruelty, that particular industrial school was where I'd resided. Such as it was, it had become my home for the previous nine years. I knew nothing else.

Throughout my years in Artane, I invariably pondered how we, Paddy and I, came to be living in that awful Artane Industrial School. Why ever did the Lady Magistrate at the Juvenile Court agree to send us into such a scathing environment where everything and everyone appeared grey, flat and with no capacity to love, where it seemed to rain more than the sun shone? Now, all alone, taking my leave, I was almost nine years, or so, way out of touch with the outside world, all due to my merciless opponents who never called fair play; the evil Christian Brothers were not unlike savage dogs, tearing at their caught hares. All such thoughts percolated through my teenage mind on that eventful morning. A little after my final breakfast and I should be outside.

Mr O'Brian who'd opened up those huge wrought iron gates all those years ago when I was seven and a bit, who had opened them for my incarceration into the Artane Industrial School, was now, the self same man, reopening them; he was causing those two main gates to yield a freedom for me. Finally, I was being let out. Noticing the welling tears in my glassy Irish eyes, he took hold of my hands in his; firmly shaking them, he stated how he sincerely wished me well for my future.

Although quite alone, cock-a-hoop, I was at least out! I was smelling freedom on a drab, wet February, yet, for me with my vivid imagination, the sun shone as brightly as on any summer's afternoon, where one would sit out and take a little Earl Grey tea in an English country garden, where the lawns were mown in lush green stripes.

Stepping out and parading along the cobbled walkways, I could hear my studded boots against those undistinguishable roads. Looking down at my happy feet, I smiled to myself, watching, listening as each heel to toe tap dance clicked out my freedom. I stomped up and down only to be sure! Various shops were lighting up their display windows which invited the locals to stop and buy. Oh, I had no money to purchase a single solitary thing, yet I could stand and stare, to simply window shop. The main thing was a joyfulness within my spirit how I was free, free from those abusive Christian Brothers, from anyone yelling at me by my number. I was again somebody. I was me, Martin Patrick Anthony Ward ... me with a hope and a future, where all the seven colours of the rainbow were in God's sky, resting in an arc down at my feet.

I needed to go on farther than the actual town of Artane, to travel into the centre of Dublin's fair city.

When I first entered the Artane Industrial School, there were street trams with their hard wooden seating. Now buses, all painted blue and yellow, ferried passengers in comparative comfort to and fro the city.

'It's fourpence into Dublin,' the driver informed me.

Hesitatingly, I stood with one foot on the step up into the bus, the other still firmly on the tarmac. 'What?' I questioned. 'How do you mean?'

'I said ...' he began to repeat himself.

'But I was only given threepence for my fare.' I pulled the old threepenny bit piece from my otherwise empty pocket, to show him how I wasn't kidding.

Due to my still wearing the obligatory Harris tweed suit from Artane, he'd quickly cottoned on from whence I came. 'Okay, son. I'll take your threepenny bit,' he stated. 'You go and sit yourself down. I'll give you a shout when your fare is all done. You'll have to foot slog the rest of the way; sorry about that.'

I was sorry, too.

I began to find a striped upholstered seat directly behind the driver, but a woman with bluish tinted hair pushed her way to a window seat. On her way in, she gave me a disapproving look which stated: 'I am an elderly person and I can go wherever I want,' and then, po-faced, she dismissed me from her mind.

After a short while, the bus pulled up with a pneumatic sigh and the blue haired woman alighted; I was left as its only passenger. The driver yelled back to me: 'You get off here, son. Will you be all right? Do you know where to go?'

I shook my head. 'I don't know the area,' I explained. 'Not at all.'

He remarked how I sounded like a local. 'Oh, look, see that road? There … see where I'm pointing?'

I nodded.

'Well, you keep on that way and you'll come right into Dublin …'

'It's the first time I've been out completely on my own.'

He begun to tell me to take care, for goodness sake, but then he, feeling a fatherly compassion, muttered something which sounded like a profanity, and he told me to sit back down. 'I am going right into the centre anyway.'

Telling him he was very kind, I twice thanked him.

He acknowledged me with the briefest of a nod.

Free and away from every sort of psychological, physical and sexual abuse, I was walking through sudden and unpredictable twists and turns, getting honked at as

I stepped out into the middle of the busy streets, yet I should press on, although I was beginning to watch all and sundry from the doorways, to shelter in them, to shield from the heavy showers which could, in no time, soak me to the skin.

I discovered a small cinema in which they showed a black and white film all about life with spindly legs in fishnet stockings. I stood agog, but I was too young to be admitted; all I could do was to imagine what it'd be like to go to such a double X-rated film with your feet up, dropping empty ice-cream cartons during the more boring love-scenes.

Being outside the Artane Industrial School assumed, for me, a lengthy period of adjustment; after all, I was in there for a smidgen under nine years, only obeying the whistle, with silence being the rule. Upon this sobering thought, I attempted to go on my way, but I'd noticed a voluptuous woman, an attractive one, maybe only a few years older than I. As she passed by, I fleetingly remembered how when Paddy visited me at Artane, the year previously, he'd brought his beautiful fiancee Mary to meet me. She'd noticed how blushingly shy I was. 'One day you'll meet someone, a grand girl for yourself,' she said, and I noticed how she was holding my brother's hand.

Paddy chuckled, saying I was too shy to say boo to a goose!

Mary offered me the advice, with a nudge: 'Faint heart will never win a fair lady!'

Remembering those words, I thought I'd wolf whistle at a passing woman. Quick as a flash, the stranger turned with a deep scowl. 'What do you think I am ... a blooddy dog to be whistled at, huh? Go on and clear off, kid!'

I had obeyed a whistle since I was a little more than seven; I was certainly no dog.

By one of the Christian Brothers, I was given the address of the Catholic Boys' Home in Dublin. Not unlike a youth hostel, I needed to kip there that night. In fact, those authorities, kind people from the Saint Vincent de Paul, made me unbelievably comfortable, so good, in fact, I remained for almost half a year; in fact, I was quite content, strangely serene.

The only person who wasn't strangely serene was a Mr Murphy. He was my cherry-cheeked employer who, when it came to me, tried hard to keep his emotions under control. He was determined not to let me annoy him; he actually blasphemed every time he encountered me! He saw me as less charming than the town's idiot, wishing he'd never agreed to take me on in his employ. Often, it'd be an adolescent moaning at length about what a dump the job was and how one can't wait to leave. Here, it was precisely the reverse as he peered at me, faintly puzzled, thinking I really was quite a fool.

A very precious parcel had to be collected from the other side of Dublin. 'Do you think, Martin,' he asked, 'you could actually be entrusted to go to fetch it?'

I nodded, pasting a smile across my face. 'Of course! How do I get there?' I worried about having to alight a bus for I was flat broke.

'No, son, you won't need any money. Take the push bike?'

'Bike?'

'Yeah. Look. See the bicycle ... that push bike over there?'

I offered a second nod.

'Yes, well, take it with you.'

Almost seven hours later, I returned totally and utterly exhausted, my sweaty red face nearly as rosy as Mr Murphy's flushed cheeks; I handed over the brown paper parcel into the safe hands of my boss.

He sucked in a breath through his teeth and swore at me which I didn't much like, not in front of the other labouring workers who saw me as a laugh a minute. 'Where the hell did you go?' he quizzed, scowling into deep forehead crevasses. 'You had the bike with you, for Pete's sake!' Although, he didn't actually say anything like those words: 'For Pete's sake.' They were much worse than that, so I made them up!

'Well,' I began, 'that was the problem; you see ...'

'What problem?'

'I had to walk with the bike all the way there and back.'

'You got a flat tyre?'

'No.'

'The chain fell off?'

'It didn't.' I shook my head once more. 'I, at least, collected your parcel, but the bike was a real hindrance, wheeling it all the way there and back, you see ...'

'Go on and tell me, for the whole suspense is nearly killing me!'

'I cannot ride a bike. See, I never learned. So, I simply wheeled it there and back, as well as lugging your parcel under my arm. Do you mind if I sit down, only for a moment?'

Mr Murphy's Irish eyes widened before tightening into slits; he was completely dumbfounded. 'Why the blazes didn't you tell me you couldn't ride the bloody thing?'

'You never asked.'

He soon saw to it that I learned to ride the 'bloody thing'! It took a while to finally balance upon the two wheels, leaving me saddle sore with bleeding knees and a scraped elbow, yet, before long, I was riding the Dublin streets like a pro.

With my day's wages, I decided to use some of it to go for a coffee. Coffee! I'd never had a coffee ... not even smelled the beverage. Although, a little shy still, I wasn't then a great talker, yet I chatted nineteen to the dozen with a cafe's proprietor; he took me behind his glass counter to show me how it was made. Oh, the aroma! If I close my eyes now, very tightly, I can still smell that first ever cup of coffee. Wonderful! I savoured it, sipping it slowly while I watched two flies copulating on the wall.

After a very long time nursing the coffee, another unfamiliar yet enticing aroma came from the the next table, infusing my senses. What was it? I wondered. I hadn't a clue. 'Excuse me,' I leaned over to talk with the owner once more. 'What's that?'

'Bacon.'

Bacon? I hadn't the foggiest what it was, but it smelled real good, wonderfully tempting.

'You haven't ever eaten bacon, son? What are you Jewish, or something? You don't eat from a pig?'

I shook my head. 'I've come from ... from Artane.'

'The Artane Industrial School? Oh, you poor kid. Yeah, have some ... can you afford it?'

'How much is it?'

'How much you got?'

I bit my lip. 'Not much.'

'Don't spread it around, but, for you, it's on the house. Okay?'

I had yet another cup of coffee and, within five minutes, or so, he brought me some cutlery wrapped in a white paper serviette; a plate of the bacon and eggs special came along with some hot buttered toast.

I sipped at the coffee, but, as I gripped my knife and fork, I stared at the two crispy rashers. I sniffed at it and continued to stare.

'Something wrong?' asked the owner with a frown. 'You want some ketchup?'

'Nothing is at all wrong. Not a bit!'

'Then get your mouth around that food; eat it!'

I didn't want to eat it straight away; I smiled in a deranged fashion, wanting to stare at it, just to see the sort of foods I'd never seen in the whole of my life. I wished Paddy was there to see it, too, but he was living his own life in the Irish army, planning on soon becoming a married man.

'Are you going to eat it now I've cooked it?' asked the man, wishing I would hurry up. 'Go on and have it while it's still hot!'

'I will, I will.' And I did. I savoured every last mouthful until my stomach felt as if it would burst. 'Thank you so very much for your kindness, sir.'

Sleeping in the Catholic Boys' Home, I awoke to a more promising day. The sun was brighter and the air clear. I made it in time for Mass and, passing by the County Courthouse where a once middle-aged magistrate sentenced Paddy, Johnny and me to Artane, I stopped at an incredibly fabulous cake shop window, a bakery offering pies filled with either cherries, apples or blackberries.

To me, it was awesome. One of the staff heaved platters of doughnuts, some were filled with a thick strawberry jam, others with fresh cream. Fat long ones were filled with a combination of both, all covered with a sticky sugar. Customers came and went, having queued, pointing to whatever they desired, and then on to the next person. They all seemed to buy as much as they fancied. When a tray was empty the server brought in another, filled up with pork pies and various sandwiches.

I'd never seen so much food; I wished I had some of the sandwiches. They all looked too delicious. Before I knew it, apple pies, Black Forest gateau, flans and heaven only knows what else came up for sale. My mouth watered at the very sight of such an array.

In my mind I kept eating. I was skinny, but I imagined that, if I ate some of those cookies, buttons would not do up on my shirt! So hungry, I barely had the chance to shovel the stuff into my mouth.

The owner of the patisserie didn't like my hanging around. 'Why do you just come and stare at my shop window? Other paying customers cannot see what we have to sell, for you are blocking their way. Go on. Clear off, boy.'

'Please, I am only looking,' I replied sheepishly. 'I truly mean no harm.'

'You don't want to buy? Then … then … buzz off!'

'I can't afford to buy anything; I am just imagining the day when I shall. You see, I've never seen anything like your cakes. Those round things with the jam; what are they?'

She knew from my accent that I was a Dubliner, but she wondered why I was so muddled.

'How come you've never seen doughnuts? Where on earth have you been? Outer space?'

'Artane. I was recently released from Artane Industrial School after nearly nine years.'

'Oh, my God!'

I told her the sort of basic foods we ate, consisting of breads, potatoes, pea soups and stews, all washed down with sweetened tea. 'I saw your window, lady, and I thought to myself, one day I'll have all the fancy breads and cakes and no-one will tell me to go away. They'll say, come on, Martin, and take your pick!' I lapsed into silence, although she heard my empty stomach rumble.

'Oh, my! I've heard about some of the goings on in there ... in that Artane Industrial School. Come on, come through into the back kitchen and I shall make you something to eat.'

'But I can't afford it.'

'Never mind all that. I can't let you starve. By the way, where's your mammy?'

I told her she was dead, how she'd died from pulmonary tuberculosis when I was four; the woman simply tutted, shaking her head and stated: 'Shame.' After making me to wash my hands, she gave me a crusty bread roll, filled with real butter and not the cheap Kraft margarine as I had in Artane, grated Cheddar cheese and some slices of onion.

I sniffed at the strange onion bulb which straight away made my eyes water and my nose run; she sort of half grinned at me. I told her: 'Not too much of that stuff, please. Whatever is it?'

She informed me it was onion. She would be making a chicken and ham pie for her own family and I would be most welcome to join them, but, shy, I politely refused.

'Another time, then?' she kindly offered. 'You want some of this fruit cake, too?' She chuckled. 'Silly question, eh?'

The woman insisted I returned the next day, before she shut up shop, and all those following days until I received my next pay packet when I had a white box all tied up with string; inside was a strawberry jam filled doughnut and a selection of sandwiches, not least with my favourite … a cheese and onion bap, along with a little note, inviting me to her family home for a Sunday roast lunch.

# CHAPTER FIVE

# "TICKLING THE SALMON"

'Little drops of water,
Little grains of sand,
Make the mighty ocean
And the beauteous land.'

Leaving behind the harsh Artane Industrial School immediately I hit my sixteenth birthday, I hadn't expected anyone to be waiting for me at the wrought iron gates, on account of my being labelled an orphan. Mammy died from pulmonary tuberculosis some fourteen years before and I hadn't seen our daddy for four years. Apart from my beloved Paddy, then in the Irish Army, and a couple of uncles near Galway, I had no-one. I wasn't even a grandson for I assumed both sets of grandparents were long gone, them and their houses in one of Dublin's grim and overcrowded estates, places where once everyone knew everyone. Those were the days when front doors could remain unlocked; nobody had anything to rob!

The Congregation of Christian Brothers who were responsible for their disgracefully tough and abusive regime, promptly passed me over to the Saint Vincent de Paul workers; the SVP men ran a happy and clean hostel, it known as the 'Catholic Boys' Home'. I confess I'd entered there with a dark sense of foreboding, yet, not for a moment should I have concerned myself; to fast forward, I actually remained under its roof for six comfortable and contented months. When I left Artane, I wondered if the hostel would be a home from home with the industrial school; absolutely not! Artane and the SVP hostel were like chalk and cheese; those godly Saint Vincent de Paul's workers did their utmost to make us boys happy, providing us with a sort of a mystical bridge between Artane and the enigmatic outside world, so very new to someone like me. For me, where the outside world was a strange environment, I valued all the help I could muster. With a new found freedom, some of those fellows saw a future where, according to our western world's temptations, they would easily get themselves into big trouble and fall into the type of issues I would have shamed my mother, had she lived. Although breathing freedom for the first time in the whole of my growing up life, the SVP volunteers performed their best to steer me onto the right pathway, as it were; the finest part of my freedom was the experiencing of the use of my name Martin, and not by that wretched five digit number of 'Twelve thousand, three hundred and eighty-nine,' to which I was forced to answer for nine years. No whistle was ever blown, and we didn't have to remain silent. It was great.

When I entered the SVP hostel, I wondered if I'd be provided with my own room. Not so. I had spent years sharing with numerous boys, boys with their own number of childish and adolescent problems. Here again, I wasn't completely alone in the Catholic Boys' Home, for other ex-Artane boys were also lodging there; I actually knew a few of those guys, they also now tasting the self same delights of freedom, having been released from that harsh institution, to where, like Paddy, Johnny and me, they'd also answered only to their own number.

The hostel became like a cushion for us and, as long as we were in by ten 0'clock at night, no-one complained. We enjoyed games of snooker; we sang and I played gramophone records I'd never previously heard. There was often sounds of loud laughter and silly jokes were told. We experienced tasty food, not least bacon, eggs and sausages for a breakfast. Between the boys there was a camaraderie in our midst; upon one memorable occasion there was raucous laughter and at my expense. I was only been a few days out of Artane; some of the lads, also free from Artane, yet before me, were also under the SVP care. Those fellows planned on going to the Mairo Cinema (formally, the Mary Street Picture House) in Dublin's Mary Street, at the bottom of Lower Abbey Street. They planned on going to the evening show, it starting at seven 0'clock.

'Come with us, Martin. You'll enjoy it,' one of the guys suggested.

I was sure I would, for I always liked films. 'What's showing?' I asked.

One spokesman informed me how it was a Roy Rodger's movie; when I knew it was showing that American cowboy singer and actor, I declared: 'It will be grand, just grand.' I looked forward to it, counting the hours.

'Fine. We'll meet you at 6.40 pm outside the "chippy". Okay?'

I nodded. On that particular Saturday evening, I couldn't express my disappointment, for not one of them turned up, or so I thought! As a result, I simply returned to the hostel and played a bit of snooker before laying on my bed with a newly found novel.

Later, when the lads returned from the cinema, they confronted me, asking as to where I was, but I told them how I'd waited outside the 'chippy' next to the timber yard.

'What on earth are you talking about? There's no chippy next to there.'

'Of course there is! There's old Tom Fahety's work shop. On the door it states:

"Chippy and joinery; enquire within".'

'But that's a carpenter's place!'

'Yes, that's right; it's a "chippy's" workshop.'

The lads stared at me, then at one and another. One began to chuckle before they all rocked with laughter; one howled until he declared his sides ached. I began to join in, but I hadn't a clue what was so amusing. Amidst their merriment, they explained the difference between a fish and chip shop "chippy" and that in a joiner's workshop. I couldn't get my head around what on earth they were talking about. They all agreed to take me out during the following day and buy me a bag of chips, then I should surely understand.

The following day caused me to be holding a bag of the potato chips. Oh, they smelled so very good with the salt and malt vinegar, yet whatever were they? I was told they were potatoes, but, how were they grown in those long shapes?

'What an idiot!' exclaimed one of the guys, still laughing until he had tears in his eyes, yet, although it was a humorous incident, it was another first encounter for me with an outside world.

I enjoyed those first potato chips; I thought they were truly delicious.

The unusually savage grey skies made way to a beautifully warm sunshine breaking through the clouds, and I was offered paid employment. Dublin was behind me and, hitching rides only from truckers, I was cutting from east to west, travelling diagonally the full one hundred and twenty-nine miles through the forty shades of green. We stopped once to refuel in the main street of a town; it was a nondescript place with a grocery store, a barbers, a pub and a place which sold farm supplies. The trucker and I grabbed some beef and pickle sandwiches as well as some pop from the garage; in his cabin, I sat beside him as he drove on through main streets, passing farms and gentle slopes of green, showing a richness in the land until we finally arrived in the party city of Galway; at one time, when I was small, probably about four or five, I was under the impression it was the place of my birth, simply because I have a couple of relatives, some uncles and their spouses still living there. I have recently been reliably informed it was Dublin where I was born and baptised a Catholic. The main thing, which I believe actually matters more than anything to me is, I am an Irishman through and through. Many folk may have had a granny or two who originated from, say Cork; others may carry the Irish middle name of Sheilagh, yet I truly can hold my head high, declaring my Irish identity and I am rightly proud, very proud!

The prospect of the paid job beckoned, providing me, I believed, with a hope and a future. In hindsight, the only sting in the tale, as far as I could see, the Christian Brothers had located the post. This news left me with a less than a warm heart for they only tended to locate menial jobs for those teenagers who'd previously resided in the Artane Industrial School; with the prospect of also seeing those blood relatives, I maintained my positive attitude.

Arriving at St James' Hotel, a red-headed woman greeted me with a broad smile. Believing, at first, I was a guest ready to check in, she began conveying her set words of welcome, saying how Ireland is also known as the Emerald Isle, renowned for its charm, warmth and loving people. From the richness of our history and culture it has a magical way of capturing your heart. Cead Mile Failtel. In other words, "one hundred thousand welcomes"!'

'Thanks for all that, but, as you can hear from my voice, I am Irish, too!'

She laughed, telling me how she'd been schooled by her boss to recite that to every guest. 'You're on holiday here, young sir?'

'Pardon?'

She raised her voice almost an octave. 'I was asking if you are on holiday.'

I believed it couldn't be a more delightful time of the year to enjoy a vacation; in early August anyone might cherish such a break away. 'Um. No,' I replied, placing down my baggage. 'I'm not, although I wish I were on holiday.'

'You're kind of reticent, aren't you? Are you going to tell me why you're here, or shall I simply keep on guessing, huh?'

I quickly blushed a deep pink, for I knew I should have informed her the second I walked through the door, but she chatted on with her welcoming speech, so much so that I couldn't get a word in edgeways. 'I am Martin,

Martin Patrick Anthony Ward and I have come here to work.'

'At last! Bring your baggage and I'll take you through to the boss.' She told me to follow her. Half way along a corridor, she slowed down her pace to grip at my forearm; in a more quieter tone, she was wishing me good luck, the luck of the Irish. 'You may well need it here, Martin ...'

Now I was worried and my guts gave a sort of lurch. To where on earth had the Christian Brothers sent me? 'I am expected, aren't I?' I asked her a little hesitatingly. 'The boss does know about me, doesn't he?'

'Yeah. I suppose so, Martin, although "he" is actually a "she"; the boss is a woman!'

'All right, but ...'

'Stop it right there! Don't ask me another thing. I'm now telling you, Martin, how I am always the last to be told anything around here.'

The whole business of working for the hotelier was a crashing disappointment. Considering the wretched Christian Brother Shannon, whose nickname for some reason was 'Segoogee' had acquired the job for me, I shouldn't have been surprised it was less than enchanting.

I started work for her as a builder's mate, helping to complete the hotel's extension. When my day's work was done, or so I believed, I was packed off to the kitchen. Oh, have no grand ideas I was learning culinary skills under the keen eye of the Head Chef; no, I was in a steamy kitchen, up to my elbows in soapsuds, washing mounds of pots and dishes. A forty-bedded hotel, I was constantly busy. I literally slaved for one hundred and eighteen hours and, although I was given food, the kitchen's leftovers at the end of my shift, I had no money. Disillusioned, what happened to that Irish good luck? It wasn't heading in my direction!

I decided to approach the woman who'd opened up the establishment, for I felt a weight heavy upon my shoulders. It should have been by then, a lovely summer's evening, yet the woman, red in the face, was hyperventilating after yelling, threatening her weak willed husband with a wooden steak hammer. The welcoming receptionist, who'd become a pal of mine, informed me how the hotelier invariably attacked her husband. He was no wife beater; the boot was on the other foot, as it were. She aimed for him!

'You'll see him regularly with a blackened eye. She has quite a hot temper, so, Martin, watch your step, chum,' the receptionist advised.

I was definitely no quitter. Although I'd had a short and not a very happy time working in the hotel, I decided to regularly relax by enjoying the occasional swim, not in the hotel's pool, but in the sea.

I had learned to swim one year while I was in the Artane Industrial School. We boys were only taken to the coast twice every year; it was there some older lads encouraged me to stay afloat by doggy paddling – before I knew it, I could swim almost like the proverbial fish! In fact, those free times making off to the sea were my most pleasant moments. I remember once how it was a gorgeous afternoon with a warm breeze; soft sunlight seemed to touch the far horizon. It all seemed so appealing. There were no red danger flags up, so I stripped under a big bath towel, donned my navy-blue swimming trunks and waded out, splashing my way into the sea. At first, it was a little chilly as my feet braved the

Atlantic waters. Onward and up to my chest in sea water, I ducked and swam; I loved it. I was free and it was all part of my new found freedom!

After swimming for about ten minutes, totally enjoying myself within the waters, I was at least fifty yards out when I thought I heard the sound of a whistle. There it was again!

Two big fellows, not unlike life-guards, were waving at me; one blew a whistle, signalling for me to swim back to the shore. In Artane everything was done by the whistle and, after obeying the whistle for nine long years, hearing one of those guys blowing the darn thing, I automatically reacted, obeying them without question.

I wiped the water from my face and returned to the beach, to where I'd left my pile of clothes. Drying myself, I asked: 'What's wrong?'

The bigger, broader of the two, his muscles rippling, declared: 'You are not allowed to swim over to the right, and you jolly well knew it, you dirty young devil!'

A devil and a dirty one at that? Me? No! I simply didn't understand. 'What are you talking about?' I queried. 'What's wrong?'

He explained I was floating across to the right of the Bay; it was to where the females alone bathe; there was also no mixed bathing on that section of the beach. 'You were deliberately drifting to ogle at the women, you filthy young beast, so go on ... get out!'

I toyed with the corner of my towel. I really didn't know I was out of order, but, had I known, well, I wasn't going to confess either my guilt or my innocence. I am an ordinary fellow with heterosexual feelings, so who knows, if I'd have stared in their direction?

Later and leaving my two big accusers, I decided to stroll along the grassy banks of the river which flowed under the Salmon Weir Bridge. Stopping by one of the fisherman, he turned to smile in my direction, to tell me he was packing up and going home. 'Wasting my time, this is, son,' he told me.

'You haven't caught anything?' I queried. 'Nothing?'

'Nothing at all, boy. For forty-one years I've been fishing in this river. It's a dour place. Now, look at ol' Tom Ward over there; he simply wades out and stands in the middle of the water and, five minutes later, you can bet your sweet life, he'll grab a whopper.'

'He's my uncle - that's my Uncle Tom.' I gave him a wave, but he hadn't seen me.

The original guy cleared off, offering some profanities as to why he hadn't even caught a tiddler.

Dad's brother, my uncle Tom, seemed to have a magical way of tickling the belly of the salmon, beautiful fish which became simply resting within the quiet shallows of the river, to just be in the right spot, at the right time. I'd once seen a Canadian documentary about brown grizzly bears catching salmon as the fish were flying up stream. Anyway, where other fishermen failed, Tom Ward grabbed only the resting fish, maybe two or three feet in length, selling them to either exclusive fish restaurants and or top class hotels; whatever a Head Chef desired, Tom could somehow provide. He said, all he did was to tickle the underbelly of the fish before they were flying up stream. Amazing, huh?

It was a good and happy occasion for me to meet up again with all my relations, particularly uncles Tom and George. They were known as a Cobog ...

country fellows, living in the small, western town of Ballygar.

As a postmen, George knew every field, every twist and turn, everyone who resided in the area. Everybody knew him, too. The local Bobby kept a close eye on him, wondering if it was him who was unlawfully distilling Poteen. Poteen, distilled from potatoes, was an unlawful moonshine – a lethal home brew! It was invariably delivered around the countryside hidden in the bottom half of a milk churn; one local farmer was told not to kill his milking cow!

George turned to me. 'Martin, come to Sunday Mass with us tomorrow, eh?'

'Am I really expected to?'

My Uncle and his immediate family paid a pew rent to the local Catholic Church, so they all had their own particular seating; our family had sat there for many generations. 'Yes, Martin,' he stated. 'You'll come with us, and in your best bib and tucker; all right?'

> 'And the little moments,
> Humble though they be,
> Make the mighty ages
> Of eternity,'
>
> (Julia Fletcher Carney
> 1824-1908, b, USA)

# CHAPTER SIX

# "SPENCER TRACY AND THE TRANSISTOR RADIO"

'The purple headed mountains,
    The river running by,
The sunset and the morning
    That brightens up the sky.'

(Cecil Frances Alexander 1818-95).

As soon as the elderly and portly parish priest declared the concluding rite with 'The Lord be with you', to which all the people automatically replied: 'And with your spirit' before bowing their heads for his priestly blessing brought down upon them; his deacon finally told them: 'The Mass is ended; go in peace ...' and the entire congregation half mindlessly chanted back: 'Thanks be to God!' before beginning to file off home. We, having sat in the front pew, were virtually the last family unit to leave the ancient building.

'Ah, now that was a lovely Sunday Mass today, Father,' remarked my uncle, shaking his hand. 'Beautiful as ever!'

The priest thanked him for the usual platitudes and, still gripping George's hand, asked in a lowered voice: 'I see you've a visitor with you today, my friend ... who is the young fellow with you?'

My uncle half-heartedly hummed and ahed a bit before introducing me to the priest, almost half wishing I hadn't turned up at all in my semi-ridiculous gear, for, to be sure, I was hardly dressed in the appropriate outfit, suitable for Sunday's Holy Mass, my sporting an orange shirt … orange, for heaven's sake, and not the expected Catholic green.

Uncle George, along with the other men of his own generation, were mostly smart in their moth-balled smelling 'Sunday best', in their well-pressed double-breasted brown suits, whereas I confess, in my blue denim jeans, various groups of women, tottering on their way out along the uneven gravel pathway to the small wrought iron gate were heard to loudly whisper and gossip. Several chatted behind the backs of their hands: 'In the Name of the Mother of God, who'd dare to come to the Sunday Mass, to turn up here today, looking more like a circus clown?' and, 'Look at him; he looks more like Delaney's donkey dressed ready for the half mile race; you wouldn't think he'd have had the guts to come to Church looking like a teddy-boy!' A younger, single woman giggled from under her feathered hat and stated: 'I think he's quite cute … poor thing, he seems a little shy. I quite like him.'

'Who are they all talking about, Uncle George?' I asked, smoothing down my black bootlace tie over the offending orange shirt.

'I'll tell you, Martin, once we are home. All right?'

I gave a brief shrug and a nod.

Home again, George wasted next to no time in collaring me and, sitting me down on the edge of my bed, he began his mini lecture: 'You really could have made a great deal more of an effort, you know; I mean, simply take a good long look at yourself in that wardrobe's mirror, Martin. Just get up on your feet and go across and see the bloody state of yourself. Go on, boy, and look.'

Doing precisely as I was told, I stared, eyeing myself from top to toe. So what, I wondered, was he getting at?

'See, lad? You could have tried to look a bit more like that fellow your auntie and I saw at the local cinema ... um, oh, heavens! What's his name now?'

'Who, Uncle George?' I asked. 'Who are you talking about?'

He couldn't think of the star of stage and screen, so he yelled along the landing to his wife; she'd been getting changed from her own posh frock into her every day frock, in their bedroom and she called back to reply: 'Oh, do you mean, Spencer Tracy?'

Of course he did. 'There see, Martin lad, when you attend Mass, you ought to be trying to look much more like him ... then you'll attract the girls, too. We'll be finding you a nice young lady in no time!'

A grin almost crept across my mouth, but I tried to react expressionless. 'Spencer Tracy, Uncle George?' I looked up at the big and broad countryman, suffering to wear his own Sunday best suit and couldn't quite see the connection.

To stop myself from saying a single word until he'd eventually had his say, he held up his hand as if he was stopping the traffic. 'Did you forget, Martin, how one dresses up for Sunday Mass?'

My lips parted, and a shaky breath escaped from my lungs as I glanced at my jacket sleeve. Unlike my uncle, I was wearing a single-breasted brown affair over an orange shirt, set off by a black boot lace tie. My trousers were also quite a poor affair, so I had donned a pair of skinny jeans, complete with six inch turn ups!

'You looked totally like a bloody Teddy boy,' my uncle persisted. 'Your auntie, well, nearly all the women on the way out of the Church, half of them were pretty inclined to disown you!'

I couldn't, for the life in me, have purchased a brand new suit. I hadn't a brass farthing to my name. The reason for my abject and adulterated poverty? The hotelier for whom I worked never paid me a single penny in all the twenty-eight weeks I'd toiled for her. I came to the conclusion how enough was enough; I made up my mind to give her one month's written notice. I shouldn't have to remain flat broke, especially considering all the hours of work I'd given for her. Actually, I had asked and regularly pleaded with her, yet all my words fell upon deaf ears, as it were.

A local judge, a well to do, gentleman, maybe in his mid fifties, invariably frequented the hotel's bar and its restaurant. He was well-known, not only in the establishment, but within the smart areas of Galway. One lunch time, I made up my mind to collar him, too, to quietly ask for his advice, as to how I could extract my back dated wages from my employer.

'What the hell!' spluttered the Judge in surprise. 'Why on earth are you still continuing to work so hard here, Martin? What are you actually doing, bloody voluntary work?'

'Certainly not!' I exclaimed. 'But whatever should I do?'

'You get here your bed and board?'

I did, yet precisely nothing else. I reckoned it was on a similar par as to when I was in the Artane Industrial

School, where we kids worked unbelievably hard, receiving no pay ... what we know now as out and out slavery.

He scratched his head and thought. 'Leave it with me, young Martin, my boy. I shall definitely have a few words with her,' he stated, reassuring me, giving a friendly slap on my back.

'But ... but, sir, what if she doesn't listen to you?'

'Well,' he threw his head back and gave a sort of a fake laugh, 'then we'll naturally take a court action against her. No problem, son!'

Intervening and true to his word, he acted, speaking up on my behalf. To begin with, the hotelier remained adamant, folding her arms across her ample bosoms with a firm no, stating how there was no point in paying me any wages as I had no means of spending it.

In all the years the gentleman Judge had practised his law profession, he'd never heard such a feeble argument. 'What Martin Patrick Anthony Ward does with his own finances is none your damn business.' he stated. 'My client has worked long and hard for you since entering into your employ.' He added how she must pay up or I should have every right to take her to a court in Galway.

Definitely not wishing for any court action and the poor publicity such issues would bring, she began to think again, and seriously so; apart from all that, she would also lose the Judge as one of her regulars in her restaurant and definitely in the bar where he was quite a consumer of a fine Irish whisky. Eventually, begrudgingly and with a forlorn effort, she stood in front of her safe to prevent anyone from spying the combination; she opened it up, paying me every last penny she owed.

At last, I had a tidy little sum to my name, thanks to a kind, fatherly Judge who cared about injustice .

Uncle George possessed an old steam radio which invariably sounded a little like a mantra as it began to warm up. There was little or no joy in sitting around, straining our ears to try to hear the aged contraption. Giving up on the family's radio, he begin to play the fiddle – taking it from its hard grey case, it was a type of an Irish viola. Although he couldn't read a single note of music, he was still quite amazing, for he could play about most tunes by ear. Once he began the music, he would start a shindig which was quite a noisy party; it would invariably continue throughout into the early hours of the morning, when even the hardiest of folk would begin to wilt.

With some of my wages, I acquired a transistor radio. I switched on my brand new possession and my uncle stated it was designed for people, for youngsters who'd already lost their minds to rock and roll. However, I listened in via the hidden microphones, the earphones over my ears.

I praised my new radio to the hilt, listening in even to the advertisements which offered everything from vacuum cleaners, to platform shoes and all that washing up liquid which was kind to your hands which became then as soft as your face. It was all so wonderful, I could hardly tolerate the mounting excitement. I twirled the dial and a voice declared: 'We'll return to our story of the day in precisely one minute after the newsreel'. Following the riveting story a Country and Western singer intoned a song full of soft romance which embarrassed me, so I twirled the dial again.

To say my Uncle George was quite enamoured by my eight by six inch box was an under statement. He kept asking: 'Show me again, Martin lad; show me exactly what it does.'

'Okay.' Turning the dial once more, Gardeners' World was in its infancy as a programme. A listener phoned into the experts, to ask what they would do with an ailing pot plant, it almost dying from its roots.

In case the listener was so monumentally cretinous, the expert suggested the plant was beyond saving.

'Yes!' exclaimed my uncle. 'All the idiot (pronounced: eejit) should do is to bury the bloody thing. No-one needs a transistor radio to be told such rubbish! Switch it off, Martin.'

I was getting itchy feet and I planned to soon move on, yet to where? I wondered. I needed to think carefully about my future. Having finished my shift, two hours sooner than usual, I decided to get some sleep; I felt bone tired.

During my time in the Artane Industrial School, we were all lads together. When we slept there was no real lack of modesty, although we did wear utility style night shirts. However, now it was all so different; when I was ensconced in what was laughingly known as my bedroom, I slept in nothing more than a single bed, in a small cubicle. The mean, penny-pinching hotelier had divided one largish basement room into three small basic cubicles, which she stated were three good single bedrooms; I was allocated the middle one. It came as quite a surprise, well, more of a shock, as I realised a couple of young women employees were residing, one in each 'room' either side of me. About ten 0'clock one night, I was tired after a long shift and I shed my clothing; having folded all my garments, I left them in a neat pile on the hard floor beside me. I snuggled down between the welcome bedclothes, ready to sleep the sleep of the gods, as it were, when I was disturbed by what? I lifted up my tired eyelids to gaze, to see to my left, feminine lace undies which were being thrown over and onto the top of the partition, to leave the clothing between her and me ... then a black and red lace bra came the other side, too, but it lost its balance and flopped down with one of the straps framing my face. Rapidly, I removed it, half desiring to examine it, for I had never before seen anything so feminine, yet I didn't dare. I didn't know quite what to do, so I simply took hold of the brassiere between my finger and thumb and threw it back to join its matching pair of panties. Its owner saw the situation as quite funny, laughing loudly. Her friend, settling into the accommodation the other side of me, called across, to ask to share in the joke.

'He got my bra!' she chuckled.

Number two woman rose up to peer over the partition, to try to take a peek at me. 'Dirty devil!' she exclaimed with a grin. 'What were you thinking of, fella, eh?'

I gave a gasp. I was trying to ignore the women's intrusions. I so wanted to protect my honour, but, stark naked, I was unable to sit up and deny any allegations. I thought it best to remain as quiet as a mouse in my wee cubicle, for, sandwiched between those two worldly wise, they were obviously up to making a meal of it, as it were. If only they knew my difficult background, how shy I was, with all my newly discovered adolescent emotions! They cared not if they spared my pink blushes; their lace undies, their black stockings, were not originally meant to tease, yet they were affecting me, like huge waves of a rough sea crashing against jagged rocks. Thinking about my two neighbours, their day clothing having been removed, I presumed they were both as naked as me. My pupils dilated with my teenage desires, my fantasies. Disrupted, I rubbed my clenched fists over my sleepy Irish eyes, half wishing they'd remove their underwear now from my sight, from on the top of the room dividers, for I was struggling to avert my gaze from all that was new to me. My pulse seemed to be racing, rapidly, with palpitations thumping within my chest wall. Surely, I wasn't having a heart attack? Not at all. I later realised they were normal adolescent emotions. I then had no idea. I gasped, so wanting to state: 'If you two don't stop it, I am going to call the local priest in the morning', and what a frightening threat that would be, for, in those far off days in Ireland the priest was a powerful being, not to be reckoned with, more to be feared than the police. I should tell them they would need time in the confessional box! But I didn't. Even so, the years in the tough Artane, from whence I recently came, still plagued me, to cause me to think in such a harsh, black and white way, with stark images chasing through my muddled mind; my hands trembled as I pulled up the covers higher, trying desperately to get my much needed sleep. Fat chance of that, huh?

The next morning, with the two giggling females gone back to work and unable to sooth my doubts, I believed it was time for me to up sticks and leave Ballygar, for I was full of a different type of guilt and gutsy pains.

I visited the busy and bustling town of Athlone, and popped into the Job Centre. This time, I promised myself, I'd acquire my own job, with my own freedom to pick and choose where and when I would work. I was still wallowing in the thoughts of total freedom well away from the Christian Brothers in that Artane

Industrial School. I discovered, though, how even freedom is somehow governed by rules and regulations; I pledged always to be an upright citizen and, as God is my Judge, I believe I kept my vow. I found absolutely nothing in Athlone to suit, so, a few days following, having said all my goodbyes, my fond farewells to relatives and friends, I planned to leave Ireland for good.

In the November of 1955, I hitched several rides to cross diagonally and back again to Dublin, to its ferry port. In no time I was boarding the B & I line, a British and Irish Steam Packet Company, leaving Dublin and docking into Liverpool.

I was dressed in a new Sunday best suit with no really warm togs, yet I needed to wait patiently with the other passengers until all the cattle, complete with a whole heap of their manure, were allowed to board first.

Unbelievably icy cold, I was seated outside, watching other passengers hanging over the rail, they all being sick in unison; they were directly in my line of vision and it wasn't too nice for me to observe.

Docking in Liverpool and, being a country boy through and through, I hadn't a clue where to go. Everyone seemed to know their destination, yet I felt swamped by the noise, all the people pushing and shoving. Picking my way through the dispersing crowd, I asked the way to the Mission to Seamen. Some shrugged, for they'd never heard of it. One guy stated he was a sword swallower; he only knew the way to a shop which sold disposable razor blades! I shivered, feeling lost in a big city. Panic seemed to be the order of the day for me until a Bobby on the beat pointed me in the right way.

'Hey, look, I'll walk that way with you, son,' he said. 'Okay?'

Arriving at a large red bricked building, I was greeted by a tall, smiling man, an evangelist with a local accent, who, after checking me in for just the one night, provided me with the most hearty of breakfasts ... the full English affair which promptly put paid to my rumbling tummy.

The evangelist sat at a well scrubbed table with me. 'What are you going to do? Where shall you go from here?' he quizzed. 'Do you have some sort a plan, Martin?'

I nodded.

'So, are you going to tell me what it is, then?'

'Wales. I am planning on going across to North Wales.'

'Wales? But how?'

I replied. 'I'm planning on hitching lifts to North Wales.'

The evangelist stared at me for a moment or two and then frowned. 'Take care, son,' he advised.

'I promise you faithfully, I shall.'

> 'I wandered lonely as a cloud
> That floats on high o'er vales and hills,
> When all at once I saw a crowd,
> A host of golden daffodils,
> Beside the lake, beneath the trees
> Fluttering and dancing in the breeze.
>
> Continuous as the stars that shine
> And twinkle on the milky way,
> They stretch'd in never ending line
> Along the margin of a bay;
> Ten thousand saw I at a glance
> Tossing their heads in sprightly dance.
> The waves beside them danced, but they
> Out-did the sparkling waves in glee:-
> A poet could not but be gay

In such a jocund company!
I gazed – and gazed – but little thought
What wealth the show to me had brought.

For oft, when on my couch I lie
In vacant or in pensive mood,
They flash upon that inward eye
Which is the bliss of solitude;
And then my heart with pleasure fills
And dances with the daffodils.'
(William Wordsworth
1770-1850, b, England).

Just a brief thought:

Wordsworth grew up in the wild beauty of Cumbria
which is quite a stretch away from both my beloved
Ireland and North Wales where I finally settled. After
travelling to Italy and France, William lived in Dorset
and Somerset before returning to his awesome Lake
District. Many of his poems describe uplifting moments
of joy which suddenly came upon him when he was
alone with nature. The sense of peace and permanence
he experienced in the natural world were proof to him
that all things – even a human tragedy – were part of
a harmonious creation.

# CHAPTER SEVEN

## "LOST AND FOUND"

'So, we'll go no more a-roving'

'So, we'll go no more a – roving
So late into the night,
Though the heart be still as loving,
And the moon be still as bright.

And the day returns too soon
Yet we'll go no more a-roving
By the light of the moon

(Lord Byron
1788-1824, b, England)

I was strolling along the promenade for what I believed it would be my very final time. That was how I had presented it to myself. I'd half believed I wanted to settle in the North Wales' coastal resort of Llandudno, because it was where my oldest sister Mary, along with my now late brother-in-law, were residing. She and Vince planned to buy their house, living and working in the seaside town, and should continue to do so for a very long time. She suggested I should remain with them, for the main industry is tourism. It meant, if I lodged with them, I could perhaps find a local job, as a carpenter cum handyman; I had learnt such joinery skills during my final two years in the Artane Industrial School. If no-one needed a chippy, then many of the hoteliers looked for either kitchen or seasonal bar staff. Then I was willing to do simply anything to earn an honest crust, for I was certainly not a lazy individual. After a few long weeks helping out my sister with odd jobs around their home, I began again to rethink my future. Maybe though, I thought, my destiny wasn't in North Wales after all and I wondered if it lay in the bright lights of England's capitol?

I honestly didn't quite know what to do with my life.

Mary began to become exasperated with my obvious instability, my restlessness, where all my fanciful ideas seemed to blow hot and cold; having enough one day she collared me and sat me down opposite her at the kitchen table. We together had a pot of tea and her home made scones that afternoon. 'Are you absolutely positive you don't wish to remain on here in Llandudno, Martin?' she asked. 'You are basically a country boy and London, even a river cruise along the Thames, would be a culture shock for somebody not unlike you.' She reminded me how much of London, like any big city anywhere, could also be a highly worrying place, with dangerous muggings and even murders.

'Hey, Mary, with respect, you've never even been there.'

She had. 'Vince and I spent some of our honeymoon in London, sightseeing and that was more than enough.' She stated how the traffic alone was like a Brand's Hatch nightmare!

Nothing, I believed, would happen to the likes of me. It surely couldn't be worse than my brief encounter with Liverpool, could it? No, not at all.

'You do not know what you are talking about, little brother!'

I became somewhat cross at being treated like a fool. If I could survive both the crummy orphanage and the harsh Industrial school, I reckoned I could weather simply anything life may throw at me. I became even more determined, wanting to reside in London, live where all the action had to be. So, that was that!

I soon packed up my belongings and pulled on a thick winter parka which Vince gave me; it was his, but it was too small for him; it fitted me simply fine. I kissed my sister on both her cheeks and my brother-in-law gave me a big hug; I promised to phone them once I was well and truly settled, but I probably wouldn't keep my vow. Perhaps I may forget? It would be simply like me to do so!

Having carefully planned my route, I hitch-hiked, eventually finding myself on the old A1, north of the capitol. From North Wales to the south of Watford, a total of three truckers helped me nearer to my destination. I felt a little like Dick Whittington minus his cat!

'Where do you want dropping off?' asked the number three trucker. 'Have you anywhere to stay?'

As yet I hadn't located anywhere, but I believed I surely shouldn't find it too hard. Then I felt a bit panicky, worrying if I would be kipping the first night upon a park bench.

'What about work? I hope you have a trade as London doesn't come cheap, you know.'

The one thing to my credit, I really wasn't scared of work, hard or otherwise, and I thought I was always a trusty reliable soul. If I stated I'd do something, then I didn't fail the person.

The trucker glanced, querying me: 'How old are you, son?'

I told him, although I very nearly lied about my age, claiming I was older, yet I didn't; what would be the point in that, huh? Apart from that, I was aware I had quite a baby fresh face.

'I have a young lad of about your age; if you were my boy I should worry myself sick.' He asked me if I had a row with my mum and dad, if that was why I was running away from home. I explained I was orphaned, that I had a brother and sisters, how if London didn't work out, I should happily return to Mary and Vince's place. I said: 'There were no bad feelings.'

After the trucker's fatherly concerns, I began to have the collywobbles, with some reservations about arriving in the smoke, homeless and unemployed. Not quite seventeen, I was half beginning to wish I'd remained back in my sister's Llandudno home, so warm, cosy and comfortably furnished. There was never without a warming square meal. However, I had set out to make it to London on the cheap and I didn't want to back out at the first hurdle. I still had enough cash for a train fare back if things went terribly wrong. Even so, I had hitch-hiked and I was setting foot in the capitol, upon its soil; that much I knew.

'I quickly need to find a Bed and Breakfast establishment, offering the likes of me a vacant room,' I told myself in a loud whisper, to find one which actually welcomed Irishmen. Those were the shockingly racist days when either many landladies or landlords might place a sign in their bay windows, stating: 'No Blacks, no Irish, no dogs'. If that was how they thought, I didn't want to stay within their dwelling places. I also wanted a pad I could actually afford, which didn't see me on the same par as a dog; that would be astonishing, more of an enigma, no, a minor miracle. 'What a cynic I could be, yet never ever a racist,' I continued, talking to myself. A cynic is a person who knows the price of all things, yet the value of nought. I didn't want to be at all screwed up like that. However, I did so desire more money for music, maybe to play on a record player, to have new designer denim jeans and plenty of fine food inside my stomach. Without a place to lay my head, I couldn't acquire a job; with no job, few places didn't want me in case I couldn't pay my rent. It was a Catch 22 situation.

I approached one Polish landlady, my trying to speak in a posh English accent, saying about jolly hocky sticks and 'what ho', but I obviously didn't do too well, for she asked me which part of Ireland I was from! I did eventually stay in a basically clean bed and breakfast room, yet it was in there all my luggage was soon stolen. I wondered by whom? Whoever it was who took my belongings, or indeed wanted to, must have been desperate! A young police officer, perhaps only about five years my senior, was brought in to investigate the theft. With only the immediate clothes I stood up in, the Bobby suggested I should check out of that B&B establishment and book in at the Salvation Army's hostel. At first, I was reticent and flatly refused, for I didn't wish to go back into another Artane Industrial School's type of a place, yet it was nothing like that. It was even better than the Catholic Boy's Home, and that was a pretty fine establishment, a bridge between Artane and the world at large.

The Salvation Army Brigadier who was on duty at the time, was a very pleasant family man, not even one iota like those cruel and abusive Christian Brothers who ran the Artane Industrial School. 'You definitely need some clean clothes; certainly, a long hot shower and a change of clothing,' he said, stepping back a pace from my bodily odour. He laughed long and out loud, for the only clean togs he could provide in my size was an old khaki army uniform, belonging to a previous army sergeant who deserted his particular regiment. Wearing it, it was a very good fit, yet, was I likely to be arrested as a deserter? You betcha! Once stepping out in the open, I was aware the deserter was still at large. When the eagled eyed police, based in London's Paddington Green Police Station, remembered their 'wanted' poster and spied me, suddenly I was pounced upon before being hand cuffed and frog marched, two officers flanking me, moving me at a steady pace.

'Left, right, left, right, left, right, you bloody deserter.' The senior of the two policemen yelled at me, as if he was still on the parade ground. Before entering the police force, the officer was in the Welsh Guards. I was also use to being marched. In the Artane Industrial School we boys were marched to all and any of our tasks. Out of step meant for us a severe beating. My present situation brought back all my terrors and I felt sick. Locked up in a stale cell in need of decorating, I was given a mug of strong tea, along with a square meal, The day dragged on with all my upsets and frustrations; I wondered if I'd have to go to a court. The last time I went to court I was seven. It was then, as an orphan, I was sentenced to almost nine years as a slave, in Artane. I looked at the thin mattress at the other end of the cell. I was permitted one telephone call to my sister Mary back in Llandudno; she was so distraught, it was her husband Vince who laughingly set the record straight and I was promptly free to go, but still in my army gear. On my way out of the station, another police officer stared hard in my direction and very nearly rearrested me; I had to find fresh civilian clothes and quickly!

Acquiring some reasonably, half decent, new clothes from the Army and Navy stores before dumping my army uniform, I soon found myself a job and started work pronto for a light haulage company. I was content, well, reasonably so, but I reckoned I needed a roof over my head. The Salvation Army's hostel was good and clean, with my sweetly smelling body odour, I imagined more congenial circumstances. That final lorry driver who'd given me a lift right into London wasn't far wrong when it came to the cost of living. Perhaps, I thought, I should seek out even a second job? I am far from being a lazy bones, so, I reckoned, bring on the hours. I'll work hard.

I discovered a room in Warwick Avenue, in the Little Venice area, right in the very heart of London. The bedsitter was about all I could afford. The loud, overweight Italian landlady who called herself Lucia, was married to Jack, a quiet Yugoslav who smiled a lot; Lucio seemed nice, telling me everyone knew her, and she was probably right, for one of her tenants chatted away nineteen to the dozen as he passed her by. The kitchenette was tiny and I could touch all two walls at once. Paying my first week's rent, I did all the things you do in such a situation – played with all the lights and plugged in my transistor radio, lined all the drawers and unpacked my belongings, such as they were. Lucio gave me three bath towels and two sets of crisp clean white bedding. Yes, this was the first time I'd had my very own pad, with my own front door key. I had, through this, found even more freedom than I ever imagined. Much behind me, having lost those sad years of growing up, now I'm finding freedom ... smelling a freedom! Yes, it felt great to find a hope and a future.

There were several others in the adjoining flats. Two of them kept themselves to themselves. When I smiled in their direction, they blanked me, simply as if I was invisible. One of them looked seriously insane, as if in a crazy world of his own. Another drifted down from her attic apartment, a little like the floaty stuff in a lava lamp.

She knocked upon what was laughingly known now as my very own 'front door'. It was the only door into my bedsitter, so nothing fancy.

'Hello,' I said, staring straight at her. 'May I help you?'

'No. Not really.'

Oh, Gosh, I thought, she must be a Jehovah's Witness. I told her I was Catholic and shut the door with a resounding click.

She banged harder. I tried to ignore her, but she wasn't going to give up, so I had no choice but to unlock my door.

Standing there with a lava lamp in her arms, she said: 'I really don't care a fig about your religion, for I have brought you my orange lava lamp.'

'Why? What for?' I took it from her. 'Is it faulty?'

'Is it heck? My lamp's completely fine.'

'What then?'

'It's a sort of "welcome to your new home" present from me.'

I thanked her very much before grinning, saying it was a pity it wasn't a green lamp. She thought I was ungrateful, not understanding between the orange and green in the beautiful Emerald Isle.

She craned her neck, trying hard to see by my shoulder. 'May I come in, then?' Before I could say yes or no, she was inside and perching on the edge of my bed, as there was little other freed up seating. She again introduced herself as the woman who lived up in the attic apartment, directly above my pad. She told me she was named Deanna, Deanna Povey.

Thanking her again for the orange lava lamp, I set it aside on a bedside table; 'I'll plug it in later.'

It was almost as if she half forgot all about the lamp, for she began staring at my small transistor radio. 'I thought I'd heard you singing, but perhaps it was the sounds from your radio, after all?'

I smiled and told her no, it was definitely me. 'Did I disturb you, for sound, like heat, travels upwards, doesn't it?'

'Absolutely not do you disturb me!' Deanna declared how I was not simply good, I was outstandingly good. 'Go on then, Martin, sing something for me. Sing now!'

'Oh, you don't want to hear any more of me ...'

'If I didn't, I wouldn't then be asking, you chump!'

Grinning in a shy sort way, I thought, wondering at first what to sing, but then, clearing my throat, I inwardly hummed to myself for a moment before offering a little from the musical: *West Side Story.

Her chocolate brown eyes widened under dark long lashes: 'My, you're good, ooh, very, very good!' she exclaimed.

'I suppose I am not too bad,' I replied with a shrug, a false sense of modesty.

'Not bad? Not bad? You've an absolutely fabulous voice!'

'No-one ever told me that before; a religious Christian Brother use to tell me to shut up and to go away, to clear off to read Shakespeare.'

'Well, by Grief, he was either crazy or tone deaf!'

---

*West Side Story (1961) is one of the greatest American musicals, adapted and inspired by Romeo and Juliet, the classic and romantic tragedy by William Shakespeare.

'Perhaps.' I half smiled for she had no idea how badly I was treated in the Artane Industrial School. I personally wasn't even allowed to be part of the Artane's Boys' Band. In their distinctive Thunderbirds style light blue uniforms with its red trim, the Artane Boys' Band were the icons of Irish music. For decades, the Band marched around the pitch at Croke Park, Dublin, and played across Ireland, Britain and the United States. Behind this image of wholesomeness lay a darker truth. Until the 1970's thousands of the youngsters in the Band were being beaten, abused and exploited at the Industrial School that gave the ensemble its name. The boys in the Band didn't receive even a penny; the Christian Brothers pocketed the cash ... the kids were unpaid labour or slavery.

Back to my new neighbour, she voiced: 'Some big shot, a musical scout should have, by now, scooped you up – it's a baritone voice; right?'

I gave a brief nod and she asked where I was from.

'Ireland,' I told her.

'Yes, even I gathered that much, but -.'

I sighed. 'It is a very long story and it's far too much to tell you about my past now.' I quizzed as to where she hailed from and she told me the far north of England, nearer to the Scottish border. She was a couple of years older than me, yet I cared not. Forgetting the age difference, I immediately became fond of her.

The most riveting thing about London is that anything can happen there. The following week a middle-aged woman, shabbily dressed, was hit by an Underground train and I saw it to take place. I was on my way to the Yiddish Strip Club where I briefly worked. They were invariably nice-looking women, in need of cash, who peeled off their gear for strangers, mostly frustrated businessmen. Back to the woman who was hit by the train, she was surrounded by commuters; she was plummeted under the train, with all its whirring cogs and gears, with the worse consequences I could only imagine.

Deanna and I so enjoyed all of our times together; we'd go out to coffee bars and drink cappuccinos which left us both temporarily with white frothy moustaches! We cherished watching either the occasional black and white film or a Broadway show, singing some of its songs together on the way home while linking arms, before hugging each other so tight and it was as if we synchronised even our breathing, the rise and fall of our chest walls. We'd started out as great chums; nothing more, nothing less until my feelings, hers, too, were in a disarray, yet I still stated next to nothing much. I remembered how I was once told by Paddy's fiancee: 'Faint heart never won a fair lady', yet I still remained the quieter one, believing we would never part.

I soon quit my job at the Yiddish Club and worked touting on the door of the famous Windmill Theatre, Soho. There was then plenty of paid work for me, for that well-known establishment never closed, with non stop reviews.

Semi-nude girls in high heels were regularly christened in Champagne. I saw many of the then famous names who received their first breaks, their first chance at stardom, not least Harry Secombe after being demobilised; he later received a knighthood.

I was always relieved to return to my room, delighted I was never mugged, even better, for I wasn't murdered! I could have been melancholy, but no, for, instead of touching both walls at once, I had spent as much time as

I dare with Deanna, and she soon told me how she absolutely adored every single and living moment we spent together. We seemed to fit, loving the same sort of music, enjoying one and another. Having been brought up in Artane, I wasn't use to the opposite sex, yet, with her, well, she was different. She always loved to listen to me, whether I was talking about my day, or singing; she made me joyfully happy, for she was a happy, smiling, fun person; she claimed how she savoured all her times with me, and I certainly did with her; the hours we spent together seemed to fly by.

When I first mentioned to Deanna we might move in together, she stated: 'I thought you'd never ask!' I leaned over to kiss her and I half wondered if she would return it, how she'd respond. The thought wasn't unappealing to me; she was so obviously more than attracted to me, after all! I loved her with a deep seated passion, yet I was heaps too reticent when it came to declaring the 'I love you' three little words, saying to her precisely how I felt, really and truly, yet soon I had allowed her to slip through my fingers; what a fool I was.

That woman upstairs, from the twelve stairs up into the attic, who'd welcomed me with that crazy orange glowing lava lamp was suddenly upsetting my entire day, no, my whole young life, such as it was, for she'd suddenly up sticks, deciding to return to Northumberland, to go back to her parents' home. They seemed to need her; but so did I and my heart felt as if it might break without her. I wanted to sob loudly as I watched her pack up her belongings. I couldn't bear to hear her even say goodbye. She'd gone and for good, yet she had definitely breathed new meanings of love into my young life.

Lucia sat me down, held my hands in hers and told me how it was better to have loved and lost, than never have loved at all, but, although she meant well in a motherly sort of a way, I so missed Deanna, the woman from up in the attic apartment; surely, she must be aching due to the separation, too?

> I felt a warmth;
> I felt aglow
> when first we met
> and said: 'Hello'.
> But, now in that warmth
> and in that glow
> there is a sadness,
> now, I know
> that we must part.
> When, after we said: 'Hello',
> we'll sometimes need to mean a 'goodbye'.
> I wonder if I'll stay with our 'Hello'?
> Yes. Let me stay with the smiles of 'Hello'.

(M P A Ward)

# CHAPTER EIGHT

# "MY LONDON HAUNTS"
# (1956-7)

"She was too young to fall in love, and I was too young to know."

There was something quite special about being in her company, for me to sit awfully close; often my thigh inadvertently touched against hers when I was upon a seat for two and I'd take hold of her hand, to feel her soft cool skin, so lovely against the warmth of mine. I claimed I cared much so very much for her, yet, no, that was untrue. I didn't only care. I loved her with a passion, but I rarely said the words of: 'I love you' she needed to hear. I was convinced how she surely loved me, too. I so wished she hadn't left in the way she had, without almost a bye your leave. Even a few days without her made me kick around at a loose end, waiting for the moment when I'd see her once more; now, I shall never see her, touch her ever again. How shall I bear our separation, for surely it had to be like a bereavement? The only bereavement I really knew was when my mother died, when I was only four; I can just about remember. Deanna's cheery face made me feel strangely warm and at peace within my present world. With her up in that enigmatic attic apartment, with our living within such a close proximity to one and another, with my apartment's kitchen walls I could touch all at once, I had a happy heart. I'd fall asleep at night and dreamt gentle dreams. She, having gone for good, somehow London, for me, didn't look either as big or as majestic. At first sight for me, the capitol appeared stately and not a little imposing, yet now the orange lava lamp seemed to offer me the only colour. Lucia's Yugoslav husband Jack tried to console by telling me I coped with life before I knew her and I should do the self same thing then, yet I wasn't sure I even wanted to. He told me I should soon recover from my wretched love sickness, meet someone else, move on and forget my first love, my one and only special girl friend up in the attic apartment. I shook my head at him, believing him wrong.

'I half wished I'd raced after her, preventing her from going north,' I stated, wondering why on earth I didn't for I now had an empty space, filling my time with a sad loneliness. It was as if I was trying to cover up a hole in my heart, yet it was one which didn't seem to repair. At the close of each day there was a void, my trying to sleep, telling myself another day would keep the dark hunger of sadness from consuming me, swallowing over the lump in my larynx.

Lucia was wise in the ways of the world, of the ways of the heart, but, although she worried for me, she thought her husband was better equip to help me, so Jack began by asking me if I knew her parents' Northumberland address, to which I shook my head. 'Well, Martin, she obviously wanted the clean break from you, otherwise she'd have left you a forwarding address.'

I could not for the life of me understand the entire situation for she had apparently loved me heaps; she'd more than said numerous times whether it was either verbally or in a note form. 'Are you really sure, Jack, she left Lucia no forwarding address?' Even if I knew her whereabouts in Northumberland, what could I do about it? Should I have chased after her? Had she desired such, she'd surely have given me some sort of a paper trail for me to have followed.

Jack shook his head, explaining Deanna sorted out her rent with Lucia before hurrying to the coach station. 'Now, Martin, I have to go and redecorate that attic, all ready for yet another tenant.'

I gave him a slight nod and planned to leave him in peace, yet prior to Jack being left to spruce up the attic apartment with a fresh lick of paint, he hesitated before glancing back at me, offering a word to the wise, as he put it: 'In future, kiddo, if and when you're properly grown up enough to meet someone nice, treat her as a lady and she'll love you for it; throw her a compliment now and again about her appearance instead of seeing yourself as God's gift to women, huh?'

Ah, he must have sized me up all wrong. I was shy, yet I always tried to think first of others. When I walked along the street with the opposite sex, I knew well enough to walk on the outside of the pavement and to stand when a lady entered a room, and so on. I did my very best. Even so, as a young man, I was fearing my own sexuality. It was unruly and always in evidence; it was powerful and threatened to overwhelm my self control. It was tricky and resilient; I hadn't expected it to be so persistent and wildly passionate. My mind prevailed over my body's urgings. I had no father's admonitions, helping me, guiding me concerning society's pressures. It was as well, I suppose, although he might have helped me handle the worrying guilt and become somewhat more sensible. All I knew about sex was what I'd been told by my equally muddled contemporaries and those paedophilia Christian Brothers in the Artane Industrial School, how sex was supposing all evil, making me then more confused. The Christian Brothers were only such, only in teaching in order to be able to practice their own perversions. Why were they so evil? Who knows?

One morning, having been unable to sleep during the previous night, Jack joked, asking if I was a vampire! I shook the cornflakes' packet and realised I had no fresh milk to go with it; in fact, my milk stank to supposedly high heaven. My cupboard was a bit like old Mother Hubbard's one. I seriously needed to shop in the nearby grocery store. In the meantime, I decided to drop in at a local cafe for a breakfast. Deanna and I were previously regulars, but only at coffee times; we used to drink cappuccinos which left us with temporary white moustaches, we laughing at each other. Anyway, I took a seat at a far window. At that hour, a little after eight in the morning, it was full of commuters. If there was one thing I enjoyed on my day off, it was wandering into town and finishing up by drinking coffee before listening to a guy teasing the waitress, but in a harmless type of a way. Even though this was the busiest time of the day, they didn't seemed phased by it. Occasionally, one of the regulars would leave a monetary tip, get up and tell her not to do anything they wouldn't with it, provoking appreciative laughter.

The stranger sharing my table, glanced at her wristwatch, sucked in gasp and left in a great hurry, as if she was going to be late for work, for an appointment, for wherever she was going. The seat was promptly taken by another breakfaster; she was no older than Deanna's age and she smiled in my direction, mentioning something to me as to how it again looked like rain. The waitress wiped the formica table, set my companion's place with cutlery and, tapping a pencil, she pounced at the ready and asked: 'You want something?'

'Sure do. I am so hungry I could eat a horse,' she declared. 'I'll have, er, fresh orange juice, followed by an omelette.'

'We have plain omelettes and cheese ones ...' started up the waitress with a sigh. 'We have...'

The breakfaster peered over at my nearly clean plate. 'Excuse me,' she stated. 'What omelette did you have?'

I was just forking at one filled with sliced button mushrooms, followed by soda bread and a frothy coffee.

'It all looks quite nice.' She looked up and told the waitress, 'I'll have exactly the same as he did.'

With the waitress moving off to yell out the order to the fat cook, my companion stretched out her hand. 'Hi. I am Maeve, Maeve Murphy.'

I reciprocated. 'I am Martin; pleased to meet you.'

'Tell me, you have another name?'

'Yes, of course.' Smiling, I replied, telling her I was Martin Ward. Sometimes it still felt a wee bit strange to say my actual birth name; even so, it was quite a delight to offer both my Christian name, the name my late mother chose, along with my last name; it was a joy to know I should never have to cry out those wretched five digit numbers, to have to answer to Twelve thousand, three hundred and eighty-nine. For the rest of my life I could boast to say my name is Martin, Martin Ward.

Maeve told me she was delighted to meet me, stating how I was not a local to which I told her I was a Dubliner.

'Oh, exactly like me, Martin; all of my family, well, most of them, are still living over there.' Curious, she wanted to know more about me, but I held back, fancying it was neither the time, nor the place to start bearing my soul to a perfect stranger; it was about then her hearty breakfast food arrived. Attracting the waitress's attention, I ordered another coffee … a frothy cappuccino, just like I used to enjoy with Deanna.

I learned how Irish Maeve worked most evenings, she being a waitress, but for a local Indian restaurant.

She chuckled, telling me how she was expected to wear a colourful sari during her working hours. 'I dress up as an Indian woman. Everything is simply grand until I open my mouth, then I sound anything but an Asian.'

We both had the following Sunday afternoon free and we planned to meet up. I was the one who suggested the date: 'I could see you under the Albert Memorial in Kensington Gardens?' I told her.

'Okay,' she agreed. 'But why shall we meet up there?'

I always enjoyed being in Kensington Gardens. It was there the Albert Memorial was commissioned by Queen Victoria, in memory of her beloved Albert who died in 1861 from Typhoid, an infectious bacterial fever. She'd truly adored her prince with a depth of a passion, and he for her, too. I wondered if the day might come when a single and free woman would fall head over heels in love with me, to think of me night and day, missing me to the point of not coping for thirty-six hours without my company, simply as I thought Deanna might have been with me.

Having left the busy cafe, I wondered if Maeve would, in fact, turn up. Oh, I did so hope she would; she was not unlike Deanna, my first ever love. She, Maeve, was more to my height. Like me, she wore skinny blue denims, yet hers seemed to almost hug her slender frame. As she ordered that mushroom omelette, I noticed a shine in her auburn hair, about the same shade as mine. I immediately liked her, feeling a tug of sensual awareness deep within my gut. Perhaps this woman was used to having men around, taking them like putty in her hand. I planned to become no putty for anyone ... no way!

With Deanna leaving me I felt apprehensive, yet I knew there should be no reverse, no turning back; forward was the only way for me, yet I desperately needed love from a woman rather than just lust. I wanted to be able to fall in love all over again, to sacrifice my heart to someone ... to a woman who'd love me with the same passion Queen Victoria had for her man. I hoped upon hope there was that special girl friend, not unlike my lost lover from up in the attic apartment.

I still worried if Maeve and I might meet, if she'd actually keep her side of the arrangement.

I had arrived much too early. I found this a little worrying, if she'd pull out of our date. Locating the particular spot, I watched a number of joggers sprinting around; some had the new headphones on, listening to the bizarre music of the stars who were rapidly becoming icons. I seemed to stand out like a sore thumb, dressed in my Sunday best dark blue suit with its murderously tight trousers. I ran a finger along the inside my shirt collar, remembering my Uncle George doing the self same to his neck during the obligatory Sunday Mass. There were two elderly women, perhaps sisters, throwing bread crumbs for the birds, but the wind caught their feed which aimed straight for my clothing! Gosh, I thought, I am going to look as if I had confetti over me; I should look a real mess for when Maeve arrives. I stood alone, brushing the sleeves with my hand.

Maeve, all full of apologies, came seriously late, yet complete with the promised picnic. 'Did you really think I wasn't coming?' she asked with a smile.

I lied by shaking my head.

'It was all due to the nightmarish London traffic – so sorry.'

'That's okay. You are here now and that's all that matters, huh?'

'Martin ...' she began, reaching out towards me. 'Martin?'

'What?' I believed she was about to say something very romantic.

'Do you know you've breadcrumbs on the back of your jacket?' She held me by the shoulder and brushed me down. 'It's as well I did this or the birds would be swooping down on you!' She thought it silly and amusing, so I offered a bit of a false laugh.

Various dates followed and we soon were sharing an intimacy. The ability to share such an understanding took still a little more learning on my behalf. Compared with her sex drive, I was still a boy in infancy; she being older than I, I felt a lack of permanency. I was still a kid, all mixed up concerning the strange matters of the heart, with no-one to set me straight..

I delighted to sing. In fact, I was passionate and I knew within myself I was a splendid baritone. One memorable Thursday afternoon I was passing London's

Covent Garden's National Opera House when I happened to notice a sign. I glanced at it, it stating:

"Stage hand wanted.

Apply within."

I entered inside and had a brief word with the doorman. 'Excuse me ...' I began.

'Yes? May I help you?'

'I have just seen the sign about the stage hand's job. Who shall I contact?'

He, taller than I, he took me by the shoulder and pointed. 'Right, sonny. Go up those seven steps, nip across the stage, then turn right. Are you listening to me?'

I nodded.

He directed me to the other side of the stage. 'Then go down the steps and, whoever you meet, ask for Mr Nuttal's office. All right?'

As I almost reached the centre of the stage, I was halted by the auditorium, by a mysterious voice asking me what I would like to sing!

My large Irish eyes widened. 'Who me?' I quizzed.

'Well, of course you. Now, go on, and tell me what you sing.'

As it was a Thursday, auditions were being held for budding opera singers, but those well equip musicians were all accompanied by their proud musical mentors, they with spiral bound sheet music. I had nothing but my baritone voice.

'What would you like to hear?' I asked the Maestro.

'Anything,' replied the expected voice.

From behind where I was standing was an upright piano. A balding head popped up from it, he, too, wondering what I should be singing, what he should play for me.

I gave a shrug. Half forgetting the prestige of the National Opera House, I stood tall, clasped my hands and began to sing: "The Black Hills of Dakota", while all at the same time, thinking I only came here for the stage hands job, not to be a singer.

The enigmatic voice voice declared: 'Thank you very much. We'll be in touch ...'

I proceeded across the remainder of the stage, only to be told the stage hand's post was taken.

Apart from telling stories, on the radio, my joy in the whole wide world is singing. Not realising Thursday was an audition day, I momentarily sang my heart out to a Maestro, a harsh music critic who'd commanded folk to bow and scrape to him, but he did at least hear me; some still say I am an Irishman with a unique talent. Maybe they are somewhat biased, eh?

I clenched my teeth. I simply had to leave my pricey digs, and also to be well away from Maeve, too. Unlike Deanna, I felt there was no future between Maeve and me, even though I reckon she more than likely had other more permanent plans in mind regarding us. It was definitely time for me to move on. I promptly packed up all my belongings, excluding my orange lava lamp and said all my goodbyes to Lucia and Jack before once again, hitching; a trucker pulled up. 'Where do you want to go, son?' he asked. Leaning out of his truck's cabin, he called towards me: 'I'm going to Wales ...'

'North Wales?' I quizzed. 'Is that where you're going?'

'Yeah. I am heading straight on as far as Rhyl's coast. No further. Any good for you, chum?'

'Grand! Thanks a million.'

By my eighteenth birthday, I'd left the city's smoke behind me, preparing to begin a whole new life, to where I believed I had a rendezvous with my destiny.

"Welcome home. Welcome.
Come on in and close the door.'

(Peters and Lee)

# CHAPTER NINE

## "THE DAY PADDY SANG: 'THE TENNESSEE WALTZ'" (1950)

'The year has turned its circle,
The seasons come and go.
The harvest all is gathered in
And chilly north winds blow.

Orchards have shared their treasures,
The fields, their yellow grain,
So open wide the doorway -
Thanksgiving comes again!'

(Author unknown)

'Hey, you there, boy! Get yourself over here.'

I gulped down the saliva in my mouth, staring up in the direction of the tall, overbearing Christian Brother. There were literally hundreds of boys, some older and many younger, all letting off steam in the playgrounds. Why, I wondered, should Brother Joe-Boy, as he was knick named, by the majority, have to single me out, of all the children? Whatever had I done to make him so displeased with me, he yelling across at me?

I was literally quaking in my boots. 'Who? Me?' I asked, rapidly examining my conscience. It was such a perishing cold day in the middle of March that I could see my breath escaping my lips as I spoke out each of my words.

The Christian Brother pursed his lips and scowled, leaving two deep furrows between his brows. 'Of course it's you, Twelve thousand, three hundred and eighty-nine. Who else would I be talking to? Myself?' He told me to get over to the entrance, to the big wrought iron gates. 'And straight away! Go on. Move yourself, boy!'

I lowered my head, my chin almost touching my chest, only raising my eyes under my own brows to see my destination as I walked every step, scared witless, racking my brain; what if I'd performed some dreadful deed, so that I was in for a really harsh punishment?

The Christian Brother didn't speak normally, but with a shout, as if all his words were each hitting the back of my neck: 'Go on, you stupid, good for nothing. Quickly now! Get a move on and do stop dragging your feet. Pick them up and march properly. Hurry up, you squirt!'

For one deranged moment, deep into the recesses of my mind, I knew those following moments, on that particular Sunday morning, may well end in heartbreak; perhaps I should be like a little luminous insect about to be snuffed out, facing an altogether rough end. I had seen such insects and stomped upon them with my boot; I certainly remember either having the collywobbles in my tummy, or my heart was racing nineteen to the dozen in the off centre of my chest wall. I cannot quite remember which; perhaps it was a combination.

Reaching the big wrought iron gates by precisely nine-thirty, I lifted high my head and looked up; there was my beloved brother Paddy in his then Irish army uniform. I could hardly believe my eyes. Full of wonder, I glazed over, choking back my joyful tears, although one salty tear drop escaped down my cold cheek, it finally falling from my chin to wherever. 'Paddy! Paddy!' I exclaimed almost with a gasp, then again with a whoopee yell. 'Whatever are you doing here? Why? Oh, do tell me … tell me!'

I do not remember if he hugged me first, then ruffling the top of my unruly badly cut hair, or I lunged towards him, throwing my young arms around his then muscular torso. He almost lifted me up in his strong arms, to swing me around into a full circle.

'Hello, my little brother,' he declared. 'I have come to fetch you, to take you out …'

I had turned eleven years old, having spent almost four of them in that harsh and abusive Artane Industrial School. For one fleeting moment I believed he was about to rescue me, removing me from that dreadful establishment once and for all. I was so excited – "over the moon", in fact! I jumped up and down. If I was leaving Artane, should I go up and collect my belongings? As if in a flat spin, I didn't know quite what I should do next.

Paddy's beautiful ice blue Irish eyes smiled towards me. 'No. No, I am only taking you out for the day, little brother. That's all,' he explained. 'Nothing more. Sorry, little one, to disappoint you.'

Fleetingly, I turned to stare up at the Christian Brother's pale pinched face; he was the nastiest of all the pieces of work, the one who looked not unlike a long thin black pencil. It seemed he was practically indestructible. He smirked, seemingly to delight in my disappointment, at my having to remain as only a number, with no first name in Artane, how I was only being let out for the day. Ah, but, looking back at my Paddy, the whole thing would have been ridiculously improbable, at my being released for good. Anyway, we were about to have a day's adventure! I exit the gate, making off with my big, strong and handsome brother, in an insane pursuit of a one day's holiday happiness.

My brother Paddy had the notion to borrow our cousin Michael Ward's pushbike. Michael then luckily possessed two bicycles. He used the one with the wicker basket on the front to run errands for small town deals, but the other was covered with an old grey blanket and half left to rust in a nearby timber tool shed. It was that same one Paddy cleaned up and made to shine; he was allowed to use it, to borrow it whenever he wished.

Paddy, following his own two and a half long years in that Artane Industrial School, had enlisted in the Irish army. That particular Sunday he'd been granted a one day's leave from the Irish defence force. Using his day's leave, he planned how he could give me a treat, a day never to be forgotten.

In a jiffy, I followed Paddy like a duckling would trail after its mother. He mounted the bike; keeping one foot on the ground, telling me to balance upon the crossbar. It was not a little uncomfortable, yet I didn't care a fig. I quickly adjusted to it and Paddy reached around the whole of my thin body, to grab the handlebars.

'Where are we going, Paddy?' I wondered if we were going to the cinema, to see a black and white film, but I was told no, not even to see the colourful Wizard of Oz. It was heaps too cold to venture to the coast; so where?

Paddy possessed a rich baritone singing voice. My own voice was beginning to squeak, to break, even though I wasn't yet twelve; I loved to sing, but, listening to Paddy back then, I kept quiet. He began to sing, to sing out his favourite, The Tennessee Waltz! With the cold March wind biting into our faces, it almost took our breaths away, yet he sang out:

'"I was dancing with my darlin'
to the Tennessee Waltz
when an old friend I happen to see.
I introduced her to my loved one
and, while they were dancin',
my friend stole my sweetheart from me.

I remember the night and the Tennessee Waltz
now I know how much I have lost
Yes, I lost my little darlin'
the night they were playing
the beautiful Tennessee Waltz".'

'That's a lovely, lovely song,' I told him, but he used the tune only to sing out all the landmarks in the city of Dublin I hadn't yet seen. He sang out all the sounds of the Tennessee Waltz to places of harmony and industry; he sang about the Clontarf, the coastal suburb of Dollymount, Talbot Street which is the principal shopping street, Cleary's department store and the River Liffey flowing into the Irish Sea. He sang to me about the timeless churches and a cathedral. We stopped nearby the famous Trinity College with its Book of Kells. I was totally and utterly fascinated by the illustrated manuscript, containing the four Gospels of the New Testament in Latin.

A few quizzical folk stopped to stare at us, to stop in their tracks, to listen to the broad shouldered young soldier, to that superb baritone on the push bike. The most splendid thing was how Paddy sang about every special landmark, which was his unique way of showing me the remarkable places, all so new to me. I felt as it was a magical experience, as if I was in a strange type of a wonderland, yet amidst such timeless places. Paddy was reopening a window, as it were, just for me. I was in a heaven on earth, but all we were was a twosome on a bike, realizing we were dealing with another scale of geography altogether, imparting both useful and useless information through the media of that memorable song.

Overtaken by a number of hooting cars and buses choking the roads, we pulled up at Mount Jerome cemetery, where, years later, I discovered it is there where our dear mother is at rest, buried following her lost battle with pulmonary tuberculosis.

My insatiable curiosity was getting the better of me. 'Oh, I do so wish, Paddy, you'd tell me where it is that we're actually going; are we nearly there, wherever it is?'

'You really want to know our destination, Martin?' It suddenly seemed strange for me to be responding again to my Christian name, to be called Martin and not just only a number.

I was busting with an inquisitiveness. 'I do! Oh, tell me, please, tell me!' I begged.

He chuckled. 'Oh, okay, little brother. We are nearly there anyway, so shall I sing it for you, eh?'

I gave a quick nod. 'Yes. Yes, Paddy, go on and sing! Sing!'

Throwing his head back, Paddy sang again to that self same tune, to the Tennessee Waltz; he sang to how we were going to spend the day with our lovely Auntie Lizzie, going to her house to eat.

Lizzie, short for Elizabeth, was our paternal aunt by marriage; she was a kind person, recently widowed, yet housing five offspring, all at home in a three-bedroomed terraced house.

Our memorable bike ride took us along the length of Sundrive Road; it was there where we resided prior to our entering the crummy orphanage. Finally, we were in Downpatrick Road where I could see some regular kids, all well wrapped up, playing out in the street, playing those timeless games of skipping, two balls against a brick wall and everything happy children have enjoyed for several generations. The youngest child was stamping her feet up and down, yelling because she was ruining the others' fun and they'd shoved her away; her mother came to her rescue and away from the older siblings' rough play.

Auntie Lizzie beamed to welcome us, yet my mind was still thinking about those happy kids all at play. I'd seen nothing like it – not ever. Oh, I wished ... but wishing would get me nowhere, or so I believed.

'Come on inside,' she told us. 'You must be so hungry - and thirsty, too, eh?'

I certainly was, but I was also extremely cold; I made my way to warm myself by her blazing log fire. It was indeed grand, a grand sight to behold.

I also kept eating. It was all too delicious to decline. Our aunt served up a chicken casserole onto white china dinner plates, followed by two large portions of apple pie and rich dairy cream. I noticed some home made scones filled with thick strawberry jam and even more of that oozing cream, so I ate one or two of those, too! There was more food than I had ever seen in all my young life! Before we left, she parcelled up sandwiches filled with thick smoked ham; there were cooked pork sausages and a whole fruit cake with eight walnuts on top. So, full of food, Paddy and I almost stumbled zombie-like back to the bike.

As we were about to depart, Lizzie frowned and looked at my threadbare winter coat. 'Is this thin, worn out thing all you have?' she asked, feeling the cloth between her fingers and thumb. 'It definitely won't keep those March winds out, will it?' She found one item that was too small for one of her own sons, so, suddenly, I had a new- to-me, hand me down coat! She pulled a knitted bobble hat over my head before winding a matching scarf around my chin and neck. She gave me some mitten type gloves, telling me to keep them safe in my coat's pockets when not in use; I promised. I certainly wasn't going to mislay those posh gloves, or so I hoped. Paddy knew full well, once I was back into the Industrial School, those wretched Christian Brothers would confiscate all those toasty warm clothes, replacing them with the regular Artane issues, and I would be left tearfully upset. However, he neither said anything to our aunt nor me. At least those new to me, new clothes would both make me happy and warm for only that one particular Sunday. I would remain warmer during the return trip than the outward journey.

With Paddy cycling back through the streets again, fringing the city of Dublin, my eyes were in awe, with our mouths open, sucking in the wind; with my crazy young imagination, it was simply like being swept along and up, up and away, flying on a magic carpet over the streets of the city of Dublin which were, by then, all colourfully lit up! It was great. The whole day was special; I couldn't believe I would have had such a good time in one very basic, yet loving household.

Back in the Artane Industrial School, everything, with the exception of the Christian Brothers, seemed grey and drab, simply all the same.

Some of my closest buddies, those of much my own age who'd nicknamed me 'Wardie' because of my last name being Ward, were keen to discover my tucker, to share my nut covered fruit cake; with a great gusto and well away from the Christian Brother's eyes, friends Duffy and Johnny ate with me all the ham sandwiches and those thick pork sausages! Oh, did we enjoy every mouthful of our contraband? Absolutely. However, all my nice warm clothes, including my precious mittens, were never to be seen by me ever again. I cannot describe my upset which was verging upon anger, but to protest would have resulted in a severe beating and I did not want that.

Many years passed me by and, in the June of 1966 when I was twenty-seven, I found myself sitting on an empty beer barrel outside an Irish pub, lonesome, grieving to the point of feeling sick to the pit of my stomach, wishing my welling tears would cease to flow. Inside the pub, beautiful Mary Ward, the now late wife of Paddy Ward and along with his three equally lovely daughters were being comforted, accompanied by what seemed umpteen mourners. Our beloved Paddy, aged only thirty-two, had died. Following a tragic accident, falling through an unstable roof, he was with us no more ... not on birthdays, anniversaries, Christmases – nothing.

With a passion, I loved my Paddy. To me, he was more than simply a brother. He was my soul mate, always a protector when I needed one. He was not unlike a father figure when we were without a parent. I could not imagine my life without him. I adored him and he'd loved me to bits, too.

> I remember the night and the Tennessee Waltz,
> Now I know how much I have lost,
> Yes, I have lost my little darlin'
> the night they were playing
> the beautiful Tennessee Waltz,

Paddy was grand, just grand!

# CHAPTER TEN

## "POPS"

'If you correct your children, they will bring you peace and happiness.'

(Proverbs 29: 15,17)

'Walk a little slower, Daddy,
said a little child so small.
I'm following in your footsteps
And I don't want to fall.
Sometimes your steps are very fast,
Sometimes they are hard to see;
So, walk a little slower, Daddy,
For you are leading me.
Someday I'm all grown up,
You're what I want to be;
Then I will have a little child
Who'll want to follow me.
And I would want to lead just right,
And know that I was true;
So, walk a little slower, Daddy,
For I must follow you.'

(Author unknown)

Previously married with two sons, along with three other step children who nestled under my fatherly wing, I am now grandpa' to six and a great granddad to a new baby girl. To all the offspring, I am lovingly known simply as "Pops".

To my inner circle of friends, I am with affection known as only Martin. Forever a softly spoken Irishman and a quiet gentleman, I nevertheless settled fifty-four years ago in North Wales; despite that, I recently heard from Arwel, a dyed-in-the-wool Welshman, say how I've the mystical title of: 'Mr Llandudno', which is absolutely nothing to do with weight-lifting! It was only the kindest way of saying I am completely accepted.

Apart from my precious friends and family, story telling and singing as a baritone are my main loves. My musical instrument is, and always was, my voice.


Inasmuch as no-one ever tries to give you a realistic view of what it's like to have children – to live with them day and night – it isn't any wonder that most of us come to the task of parenthood naïve, poorly prepared, with mistaken expectations and wrong training.

Having babies sounds like fun, pretty and playing in either pink or blue in a beautiful nursery, never making the mistakes our mothers made. So much for the fantasy.

The reality, like most of life, is a bit more complicated. It certainly was for me when I was a child, subjected to the lack of parental love and guidance, having only yelling, anger, causing me pain, much pain in mind, body and spirit; the latter was being crushed twenty-four hours a day, seven days a week when I was tired, when I was ill, when I distracted and weak. Those sadistic Christian Brothers were strong, demanding and unpredictable. They were feisty, fully formed adults, aware of plopping into my world, taxing me to my limit.

From deep within my soul, deep within my spirit, I knew I could sing, yet the Christian Brothers, usually the infamous Brother Joe, tried to forbid me to be at all musical, telling me I'd be better occupied learning Shakespeare! Why him, for goodness sakes, I do not know to this day.

I remember, as a daddy, sitting up through the nights, pacing the floors, with my kids when they were fretful, singing a lullaby softly to them, gently, lovingly until they were calm. It was natural for me to rock my babies, singing, yet, as a child, I was forbidden to sing. In my head, in my heart, I longed to sing; my voice broke early. I was no more than twelve, showing signs of becoming a baritone, not unlike my big brother Paddy.

My mother died when I was four and I am sure she would have loved me so very much, but it's hard to be left behind. To this day, I regret losing her, but, once in the orphanage, then Artane, I lost the enormous wellspring of my own capacity to sing. When I left Artane the mystical walls, as it were, like those in Jericho, came tumbling down and my voice won through, lovely and permanent with a full inspiration.

Now, in my adult life, I'm not only faced with the smatterings, but with tasks which seem too monumental to contemplate. I have overcome difficulties like the old man in the old poem "who tackled the task that couldn't be done, and he did it".

William Blake said: 'Great things are done when men and mountains meet'.

Therefore, as a man, I conquered my mountain, as it were; back in 1963 I first sang to an audience, a Welsh audience at the Craigside Spar Hotel, Llandudno. I wasn't even the slightest bit nervous, and neither were they! I was simply thrilled at being asked. Before venturing to Wales, I sang throughout the pubs and clubs in and around London; it was in the big smoke, I entered a number of musical competitions. Did I always win them, hands down? You betcha. Many of the clubs had the climate and ambience of the wealth and style of the big London city. I was enchanted, yet I'm happy here in Llandudno even when the promenade is crowded with sweaty pedestrians and shuffling tourists, when the sun is warm on my back, when almost perfection abounds.

In 2008 I discovered how the manager at Tudno FM107.8 (local radio) was looking for a DJ, to have a four hour's slot on a Sunday, starting at ten in the morning. I applied. Now, every Sunday, after playing a few minutes of the Big Band Sound, I begin by saying something to the effect: 'Hello and good morning, it's truly a lovely day; the sun's only above the clouds … in between the rain drops, it's bone dry! I'm Martin here in the "shed", as ever. Sure to goodness, it's lovely to be here; it's probably snowing in China - who knows? But not here! I hope you are all healthy. And, as for the time, we'll only know that when the news comes up. In my haste, I forgot to bring my watch!'

I played a track of the late Guy Mitchell singing: ' She wears red feathers in her huly-huly skirt' and I began to wonder about the poor, now bald cockerel. He'd normally be strutting around the farmyard, the pride of the hens' place, now minus his magnificent plumage, for all his red feathers were in someone's huly-huly skirt!

After playing Vera Lynn singing: 'The nightingales sang in Berkley Square' I threw out to the listeners, asking: 'Whatever happened to the nightingales - who knows?' And, blow me, the very next day someone who is a near neighbour, e-mailed me at great length, informing me all she knew about those birds!

It doesn't matter if it is blowing a hailing gale outside or plain drizzling, I offer, in the brightest, top of the morning in my softly spoken Irish voice, how it's a lovely day, how everyone should smile when they wake up, remembering it's their day off!

Speaking of the weather, I told of my umbrella which had holes in it; why did it have holes? Well, if it didn't have the ubiquitous holes, how would I know if it was raining, or not? A friend heard my strange reasoning and decided to have none of it; she promptly purchased me a spanking new telescopic brolly!

One Sunday morning I was asked, no, told to read the news. I quickly glanced through the white sheet of paper and, having given a brief cough to clear my throat, read: 'It was announced today how the internationally famous Reggi King has sadly died and his funeral is to be held on Thursday.' Folk listening were wondering who on God's earth was Reggi King. Three times I had read exactly the same until ten minutes before one in the afternoon I was corrected by the powers that be, telling me to read and to re-read the wretched thing, although they didn't use the word 'wretched'! I made that up. It wasn't anyone going by the common name of Reggi King, for it was the 'Reggae King' who'd passed away; reggae is the West Indian style of music with a strongly accented subsidiary beat. Anyone going by the name of either Reggi, Reggy or Reginald King - well, I should have apologised, but, not at all, for I simply blamed the little leprechauns!

It wasn't long after that memorable incident when the local radio manager asked me to interview the local fire officer. All went well until the end of the chat when I asked him how folk could contact him, if they so wished. He promptly replied how they could either fax or e-mail him.

'And if they can neither fax nor e-mail?' I asked, 'what then? Do they simply send you up smoke signals?'

I could hear Andy, my then radio manager, inwardly groaning to himself!

More than once, I didn't know how to switch over to the news, not at ten, eleven, midday and at one o'clock, so I just laughed it off by declaring: 'Ah, well, no news is good news!'

There were occasions when the more gullible listeners really believed there was an old granddad named Boris with his rear end stuck in the ice, in the Russian Urals, how there is also an entomologist based in a rain forest hut who cannot leave his cabin for the squelching mud, yet now a 'Steve the pole dancer' has made an appearance; no-one much believes me how this Polish man exists, despite whatever I say in my own defence!

Day by day began to seem uneventful. Everything was jogging along fine. The celebrations of the New Year came and went. There was nothing much new, or so I thought, until early in that same year of 2010, I was removed from my comfort zone by the management at the local radio. It was one of those bods who expressed how they required three volunteers. Colleagues Kevin MacArdle, David Jones Jnr. and myself were being singled out ... to be the chosen few! Chosen for what, we wondered. We three were actually selected to attend a 'Celebration of Volunteering' and in the presence of the Queen and Prince Philip.

How exciting, I thought, wondering when it might be. However, my raise of excitement took a nose dive; we heard nothing more for what seemed ages. Life resumed its usual hum-drum until our three names were sent to Her Majesty's Lord Lieutenant of Clwyd, Mr Trefor Jones CBE. Once more, my excitement began a wow, to bubble to the surface, especially as we three buddies were told we'd been selected from many.

An official instructed Kevin, David and me as to what we were supposed to do when confronted by Her Majesty, how to answer questions, and how to know when she'd had enough of listening to us.

All too soon it was my turn to face her, for the day had come.

Suddenly, she was standing before me. Did I call her Ma'am to rhyme with jam, or Ma'am to rhyme with arm? I simply couldn't remember; if I said the wrong thing, I'd carry the error to my grave. I knew I would! She was shorter than I imagined. Her features were a carefully composed mask and my eyes held hers for a few timeless moments.

'Who are you?' she asked.

I thankfully remembered my name, adding the words of Tudno FM: 'I am a volunteer for that local radio station.' I think I said a little more, yet I forget as to what.

'Oh, really. How interesting. Have you been with the radio for long?' she quizzed.

I began to tell her about my two years with the radio, but, before I knew it, she had moved on to Kevin and David, the latter, thanking her for coming, hoping she and Prince Philip would have nice day.

During the afternoon the Royal pair sat through a festival of musicals. The youth showed Andrew Lloyd

Webber's musical: "The Likes of us". He actually made the short musical for the Queen, yet it never saw the stage until 2005. The Llandudno Youth Music Theatre showed the life of the Irish philanthropist, Thomas John Barnado. The Youth sang a medley from "The Likes of us", not least 'Have another cup of tea' from Act 2; the Queen and her husband clapped!

The day completed with the singing of the Welsh National Anthem, prior to our Queen and the Prince meeting the flag waving crowds lining the promenade.

In the month of July, 2013, I spent three days in Dublin. In various ways, quite entrancing among a little of some of my family memorabilia, I'd only taken a mini vacation; I'm happily returning in a couple of weeks to enjoy a quality time with my family. I plan to return with the undeniable convenience of a place which, apart from the Artane Industrial School, makes me proud to be an Irishman. The weather, oh, the weather, despite being in the very heart of a July summer, was unsurprising wet. The forecast gave out how there would be a few scattered showers. Well, I do not know where they'd scattered them, but, where I was staying the heavens opened and the rains came down like a curtain. The dark clouds dumped even more down in bucket loads, throwing in some forked lightening for short measure; I was transfixed. As I took shelter and stayed as dry as a bone, I was more than a little amused to see the pedestrians running in all directions, to avoid a soaking through to their skin! For once I was relieved not to have my umbrella with the holes, despite it being a fine talking point! Having boarded the ferry back home, back to North Wales, it felt cosy, good, snug and quiet, nice to be again in my own bed, to be in my own place where I'd be safe, to simply please myself,

In Llandudno it seemed it was a year without much of a summer, with a spring emerging into a drab autumn. With dull, grey skies, with the drizzling rain soon changing into sheets, it was like having a power shower. Upon the rare occasions we did spot the sun in its intensity, briefly dazzling, locals were hysterical; I squinted with the unaccustomed brilliance before it wintered all over again.

Apart from chuntering about the weather, it became my intention to retrace my family tree, homing in upon my late mammy's life, in Ireland's County Clare, with the whole sequences tattooed on my memory. Always anxious to climb up and through the history of the clan with its unique tree, I was not a little surprised I kept coming up against odd twists and turns, along with abrupt T-junctions, requiring me to go left here, then right before left again, and so on, half believing I should never really know about her and me. This seemed a great, tear-jerking pity until some Pennsylvanians popped up, orientating me with some new tales, pointing me into a thicker monologue, along lines witnessing the original story concerning the landmarks, leaving me to ceaselessly fidget, to half drive me crazy, distinguishing me to eat up all the names, dates and guiding me through a past life where I tended not to linger. I so needed to know those previously unknown to me, folk who'd firmly declared they were my long lost cousins.

I live in a ground floor apartment. So excited, I locked my front door and rushed up the twelve stairs into my neighbour's pad, a great smile having crept across my face, anxious to share my news, yet not before she made me a mug of coffee. I rarely enjoy her tea, decaffeinated or otherwise.

Telling her about my new found American cousins, I informed Jan: 'I have decided to go out, to meet those relatives.'

Performing a sort of double-take, Jan flopped herself upon the sofa. 'What? You're surely not going to fly out to the States and all by yourself?'

I shook my head. 'I shall go in a plane!' I joked.

She didn't even smile at my jesting, but sucked in her breath, simply as she always did during uneasy moments. It was then she told me in an apologetically way how it might be in a rough neighbourhood where one stands in line to be murdered, as in New York where there's a murder every four hours. She was obviously trying to stop me from going on my own, to prevent me from encountering those enigmatic strangers. 'As they want to meet you so much, too, then why don't they pay to come over here, to Wales? Oh, yes, and another thing …'

'What?'

'How'd you know they're not a bunch of weirdos?' Jan offered one obstacle after another, but only out of a concern. 'They might kidnap you.'

'Now you are just being foolish!' With all my resources and intelligence, along with a deadpan attitude, I was even more determined to fly out to Pennsylvania without incompetence, with total enthusiasm, meeting any obstacles head on, settling with a nice warm feeling in my heart of hearts.

Jan still didn't like the idea of my flying out alone.

'Have you never flown alone?' I asked her, knowing she'd spent a large chunk of her professional life in Ohio, in Amish country where there was nothing much more than a general store outside where old guys swapped tall stories and spat in barrels; Mennonite homes with white clapboard stood incongruously by drive -thru banks, places where gob stoppers were given out, where nobody got briefly excited. It was away from the big city where no-one went for walks, for everyone drove, even to the next block.

'It's a city where I shall be,' I told her.

'What?'

'Bethlehem ... that's the name of the Pennsylvanian city where I shall be.'

'Walk anywhere alone and the cops will pick you up.'

I like walking. I am a country boy and I planned to walk places.

'Please yourself, Martin. Remember the American cops are armed. They're not quite as accommodating as our police. Oh, yes, you'll need health insurance.'

Through my clenched teeth, I firmly declared I had health insurance, but I wouldn't need it. Nothing would happen to me.

'You fell over when you were in Dublin. You cut your head and injured your left shoulder.'

Both Jan and many of the adults in my immediate family hadn't allowed me to forget how I fell over on my way to the public house. When I staggered in bleeding, the bemused publican remarked how most guys left bleeding; they didn't fall on their way into the pub!

Jan told him: 'As it's a long haul flight, you'll need flight socks.'

'Why?'

'So, you want a deep vein thrombosis?'

'No.'

'Buy then some flight socks ... and when you are up in the air, move around and wiggle your toes.'

Anything for a quiet life.

'You'll get jet-lag, Martin. You'll find yourself sleeping at odd times.'

'I shall not.'

'You shall.' She added how I needed to have on hand the exact address of where I was staying or I wouldn't be admitted into the USA, but I didn't hear. It was either that or I did not wish to hear any more instructions, eh?

Preparing to enter the USA is certainly not the easiest country.

'I already have a visa,' said I.

The events of 9/11 have made entry more difficult than it use to be. For most purposes, the majority of travellers need not only apply for a visa, but have a simple visa waiver to complete when actually in flight and prior to landing.

I was told all this, but did I listen to Jan when she reminded me of my needing the full address of where I would be staying? I simply smiled and said I'd be fine. I should be staying with my cousin in Bethlehem, Pennsylvania. Simple.

'E-mail me, Martin, when you arrive. I'll want to know you'll be safe and sound. I have told you how I worry about you.'

'I know. And I shall wrap up warm, too!'

'Yes. Well it is very cold out there, especially at this time of the year.'

I told Jan she was like an old mother hen. I like the cold, yet she added it was icy cold. 'Why do you think the brown bears are hibernating?'

On the twenty-fifth of November, 2013, I left the drab weather in the UK, flying from London's Heathrow Airport and arriving into Philadelphia's Airport, bringing many of the passengers into a fever pitch of excitement, those who were arriving home, others who were not unlike me, visiting Uncle Sam, yet they for various and other reasons. Leaving the sardine packed craft, I saw a sign the size of a battleship with a huge arrow telling us to turn left for immigration and get in line, a half a mile queue where we would penultimately end, almost to where the one guy in front of me smelled like a long dead horse, emitting mournful noises.

Waiting was like a double dose of Valium and I wondered about my luggage on the carousel; it finally became my turn when the overweight customs' officer's beady eyes began to look me over with a sort of casual distain. I stared straight back with a look which conveyed a warm heart and innocent demeanour.

'How yew doin'?' he asked, as if he really wanted to know about my welfare.

This so astonished me that I answered in a softly Irish tone: 'What?'

'I said: "How yew doin'?"'

'I'm grand,' I replied, 'just grand.'

'Y'on vacation?'

'Yep.' Then I rapidly changed my mind, for of course I wasn't holidaying in the USA. No. The fellow was perhaps armed and I couldn't quite comprehend a single word he was saying. He did not repeat himself, but asked about the full address where I'd be staying, especially my first night in America. The guy remarked how my visa waiver form, completed by me during the flight, didn't show the whole address to where I should be residing. 'I am staying in Bethlehem.'

'Yew kinda slow, ain't yew?'

I shook my head, regarding myself as bright as a button.

'Where in Bethlehem? What is the exact address, huh?'

Jan's previous words haunted me as I recollected she'd told me how I'd need the full address, yet I hadn't the foggiest when the American changed tack, quizzing me as to whom I was staying.

'Relatives.'

'Yew know 'em well, eh?'

I shook my head. 'I have never met them.'

'And you don't know what number, which street? Tell me what you do know concerning their whereabouts.'

'I dunno. All I do know is that there's one of them waiting outside for me; she'll be wondering where I am.'

Believing me, I finally was photographed, my fingerprints taken and my passport was stamped; I was free to go, but not before he stated: 'Next time, 'fella, have all your details. Okay?'

Next time? I thought, I shall remain at home. Never would I suffer that rigmarole ever again.

Kathy, accompanied by her husband of twenty-five years' marriage, drove me through the evening sunshine. Here and there the snowy roads led passed collections of pine forests and, after only a few hours' drive to the city of Bethlehem which seemed to have everything you could desire, in where the folk were as excited as schoolchildren on a trip, none the less absorbed by me, their long lost cousin from the "old country" and to them I was the "Darnest thing", they leaning over to talk real perky. Whatever, I had to constantly remind them I was there to find out more about my mother, Annie Mac Mahon who came from County Clare, they upon the self same search.

During my time in Bethlehem it was Thanksgiving. I lost count as to how many folk gathered around to devour a couple of roasted turkeys, with us all seated together at one big table, I had never seen so much food. It was all so delicious and pretty soon all the guests knew all about me. We all had a great time. When my plate was nearly empty, Kathy saw the food kept coming. I kept eating. It was too delicious to pass up, yet had I consumed any more turkey, I thought my trousers wouldn't fit. I finally stumbled zombie-like to my room into the night where I was desperate to sleep, moaning softly. After homemade apple pie and ice-cream, I was almost too stuffed to speak, yet my hosts were anxious to hear me sing Irish songs from the land of my birth. I was the first real live Irishman they'd ever met, to this they gave a whoop of joy, offering me a cup of coffee with cream, cream instead of milk.

They were the friendliest of folk, but I made the mistake of saying thank you. 'You're welcome,' one said. Once you start this there's no stopping them. I asked for a glass of water and they smiled at me; it was all rather unnerving.

'Thank you,' I declared.

'You're welcome,' one would say in a sing song voice.

I simply smiled sweetly. Every time I took a sip of water, another would come forward and top up my glass. 'Thank you,' I would add.

'You're welcome, cousin Martin.'

After a whole heap of coaxing, I finally gave in and sang:

> "The pale moon was rising above the green mountain,
> the sun was declining beneath the pure crystal sea;
> when I strayed with my love to the pure crystal fountain

that stands in the beautiful vale of Tralee,
she was lovely and fair as the rose of the summer,
yet 'twas not her beauty alone that won me;
oh, no, 'twas the truth in her eyes ever dawning,
that made me love Mary, the rose of Tralee.
The cool shades of evening their mantle were
    spreading
and Mary all smiling sat listening to me;
the moon through the valley her pale rays were
    shining,
when I won the heart of the rose of Tralee.
She was lovely and fair as the rose of the summer,
yet 'twas the truth in her eyes ever dawning
that made me love Mary, the rose of Tralee."

Everyone clapped and my cousin Delores called for an encore, but I firmly shook my head, telling them I'd probably sing again for them another time, another day, for I was feeling zonked, too weary, anxious for some shut eye.

Despite what Jan informed me, how no-one walked anywhere, I went for a stroll around Bethlehem, that is to say I walked up one side of the street and down the other. A few people smiled as I passed by. Feeling vaguely homesick for those dear to me, missing those who love me in Wales, I gave those I passed by the same eerie smile, concerned I might encounter a brown grizzly bear, a real live hungry bear. One such greedy animal ventured into Kathy's garden, anxious to fatten himself up prior to his hibernation, during the long cold winter. By the way, no armed cop stopped me from walking! No cop was anywhere to be seen; perhaps he was tracking down either bears or robbers, screaming at them: 'Okay, hold it right there, buddy!' Either that or more likely he was viewing the ball game on the television.

The ten days in Bethlehem, some of which were with my cousin Delores, others with her kind daughter Kathy, were novel experiences. They were wonderfully precious days I shall always hold dear. With a sinking heart that was it. Approximately five thousand miles away from home, a childlike voice in my head cried out: 'I wanna go home!'

Saying my fond farewells even to one of the house dogs which sniffed at my feet, Kathy drove me to the Philadelphia Airport. A sign ahead declared: "Buckle up. It's the law in Pennsylvania." I buckled up!

In 1587 a group of 115 English settlers sailed from Plymouth and set up the first colony in the New World. Four hundred and twenty-six years later, I was desperately anxious to leave. Now, if those settlers had a few issues, it'd be a walk in the park, as it were, simply for me to board a mighty great plane, to fly back to London's Heathrow and onto Manchester Airport. No problem. Hey, but we are talking about yours truly and no-one else!

First, I acquired my boarding pass, which showed no gate number. Treated as if I was some abandoned hillbilly, a cheerful beauty in a neat uniform sat me at Gate 17. I seemed to sit there for so long that I swear my usually neatly refined beard grew longer! An hour and a half later I became suspicious I was in the wrong place. I could no longer sit naval gazing, so I spoke up in a clipped voice to a smartly dressed young man, asking how much longer I'd have to wait, to which he said he was sorry and sent me to four gates further on, to Gate 21 where my flight was being called for the final time.

Thankfully, I do not carry any excess weight upon my person, hence I was fit enough to just run in time to catch my flight. At least there were no issues returning back through customs; I jolly well knew the address where I'd be going, where I would soon be, tucked up in my own cosy bed. At least, so I thought.

Unbeknown to me, Kathy, back in Bethlehem, was e-mailing Jan to say I had left behind several pairs of pants and a few shirts. Kathy asked Jan to let her know if Martin arrived home all right, that she'd send on his pants, and so on. Now, I knew Martin had acquired several more pairs of Y-fronts; he broadcast it over the radio's airwaves, requesting if any listeners knew where he could buy some! Kathy laughed. No. Not underpants, but by pants she meant 'trousers'.

While all this was happening, the plane in which I was packed in like sardines, was delayed. The Captain announced the delay would be for fifty minutes, but, in fact, it was for two and a half hours. I tried to contact my friend Terry. He was to meet me from Manchester Airport, but the messages became mixed so he drove home without me. Landing late and now alone and bone tired, I was informed the railway was stopped due to floods on the line, but I was told I could get a coach. I tearfully watched the coach drive away without me. Now what? A number 12 bus made it to Llandudno Junction, stopping at every stop on the way, via Rhyl. With all my luggage, minus a few shirts and trousers, it would have been quicker to have travelled by Delaney's donkey for then I had to discover a way to travel from Junction to where I live on the West Shore! I finally turned the key in the door, letting myself indoors. At 8.45 pm I let Jan know I was safely home; in turn, she reassured those in the USA.

A few days later, Jan stared at me and said: 'You have jetlag, Martin.'

Fast asleep at all the wrong times, jetlag definitely demonstrated itself, despite my stating I was grand, just grand!

In the following Sunday, I looked out of the window to discover what kind of a day it was. It was a great day. I showered, dressed and ate the briefest of breakfast; I burnt the toast, setting off the wailing smoke alarm, a noise which could wake up the area.

By ten in the morning, with a happy heart, my own radio show came on air. When I say I had a happy heart, I wasn't exactly turning cartwheels, you understand, but I was leading various listeners back in a time, way back down their own particular memory lane, as if they were young again when every turn in their path erected an exotic surprise, a grand adventure, passing over those lost generations.

I happily wandered through the four hours without seeing a single soul, yet, it was overwhelming to connect with a whole volume of worldwide listeners who, believe it or not, couldn't do without me, their regular Sunday fix, requiring my show as much as they need fresh water upon the earth.

No-one ever invites me to have a nice Sunday luncheon meal with them, for I invariably broadcast how I'll be dining with one or other of my relatives. Whichever one feasts me, I plead with them to give me a small portions; my words seem to fall upon deaf ears. They plug into my fists a knife and fork, ready for me to lunge into enough food to satisfy a horse, or at least Delaney's donkey! Every time I plead no more, more seems to arrive upon my plate.

My friendly neighbour Janice whose imagination is only surpassed by mine, thought about old folks opening their curtains to only see the grey gloom of a dense fog! Despite a blanket of fog, drizzle, strong winds and maybe even snow, they'd twiddle the dial on their on their little radio, just by their bedside, and hear me destabilise the judgement of the listeners, as I declare: 'Good morning ... it's a lovely day today ... a day when it's good to be alive!'

The self same friend imagined an old grandfather plodding in his paisley pyjama's bottoms over to the window and, peering out, he couldn't see a darn thing, just a pea souper fog, so he climbed back into bed with grandma', remarking to her how it's a bit grey outside; he tried to go back to sleep under meticulously ironed sheets until he's shocked into wakefulness by a buzzing, a roaring and the clock-radio-cum-teasmade was reacting to its time set; it was on the mantelpiece in their bedroom. Across the airwaves, he hears a cheery voice declare: 'Good morning. It's a lovely day. The sun's only to emerge from the clouds and, by golly, it'll be a lovely day ...'

Covering his head with his pillow and, with a kind of a dull shock, he moans: 'It's that bloody Irishman again!'

The grandmother leans over him. 'Oh, but I so like Terry Wogan!'

As the sun goes down, filtering through the trees, throwing long shadows across the lawns, with a pleasure, I think about putting my feet up at the end of a busy Sunday, but I suddenly remember there is some proof reading concerning this ever expanding manuscript; what do they say: 'No rest for the wicked!'

I was quizzed by a buddy: 'What's your favourite song, Martin? If you were marooned on a desert island and you could only take one song, what would it be?'

I replied how there are so many songs, so many I love, yet, if I was really forced to decide, I should probably declare: 'In a heartbeat it would have to be "Fields of Gold" by the late Eva Cassidy who died young through a skin carcinoma. It's a very special song; a friend and my neighbour invariably requests this piece to be played this over the radio. If it's not that, she is asking me to sing something Irish over the airwaves!

'Fields of Gold' is about two lovers, soul mates; it is also quite a spiritual song. He, the male lover, married later as the woman nears to her death. She returns to where she was most happy in her life. Their love was worth more than gold. It describes falling in love, and how exciting must that be if it's the real thing, huh? They both swear their life together has to be forever.

> "Will you stay with me, will you be my love among the fields of barley?
> We'll forget the sun in his jealous sky as we lie in the fields of gold.
> See the west wind move like a lover so upon the fields of barley
> feel her body rise when you kiss her mouth among the fields of gold."
>
> ('Fields of Gold' by Eva Cassidy)

# CHAPTER ELEVEN

# MAKE THEATRE HAPPEN

"There's no business like show business like show business
I know, everything about it is appealing, everything the
traffic will allow; nowhere could you get that happy feeling
when you are stealing that happy bow."

(Irvin Berlin and Ethel Merman).

I had slept fitfully. I finally awoke some moments before
the bedside alarm would have sounded its irritating
bleeps. It didn't matter for what time I set the alarm,
I always opened my eyes before it sounded. Don't ask
me why. I dunno. All I do know is it was then I could
well have curled up again, sinking back into my comfy
pillow; I felt unbelievably tired. For a short while
I remained motionless, quiet, thinking about the day
stretching out before me; the previous day's weather man
on the BBC promised it to be a scorcher. I eventually
swung my legs around from the bed and padded my way
across to peep through our bedroom curtains. I wiped
away the condensation from the window pane with the
side of my clenched fist; I looked out. A Mediterranean
type blue sky was evident in North Wales and without
a single fluffy white cloud crossing it. I began to shower,
sending the pipes into spasm, shaved, dressed quickly
and made it down to the kitchen before any of my family

had begun to stir. A few miles out of Llandudno and I'd be crossing into the neighbouring coastal town of Colwyn Bay, yet, I believed I needed to glance through my part in the script, and for perhaps the final time.

The previous week, it was during the final dress rehearsal when a close friend and a fellow thespian began to remark with a grin: 'Hey, you'll never know, Martin ...'

'What?' I interrupted. 'What shall I never know ... I'll never know my lines well enough? Oh, heavens above! Is that what you were about to say?' Suddenly I was worrying to the point of panicking deep down in my gut.

He shook his head and then offered a forced laugh, telling me to shush and to calm myself down. 'No. Not at all, Martin, old chum. All I was about to say was you'll never know, my friend, if some influential talent scout from either London or even New York might be in the audience; if they were, they'd scoop you up in quick sticks, offering openings even on Broadway for a guy with your outstanding acting abilities!'

'Are you kidding me?'

'No, of course not. Why should I do such a thing?'

I shrugged my broad shoulders. 'You are either flattering me, or you are totally biased.'

'Neither. Anyway, Martin, if something like that happened, well, then the world would be your oyster, eh?'

Blushing a little pink from the neck up, and simply only to display my wave of false modesty, I replied by asking him which planet he was from - Zog? Even so, deep down in my heart and soul, it would indeed be a delight to advance my stage talents, to be also even more well known for my strong singing voice. Not unlike my brother Paddy, my voice was baritone; it broke early, at around the age of twelve years. However much I loved singing, it was dashed by the evil and abusive Christian Brother in the Artane Industrial School, he telling me I had no talent, how I'd be better learning Shakespeare. Those words from my childhood had remained within my psyche. However much folk tried to convince me I had a superb voice, I remained unsure.

Whatever, I was to play the infamous Jud Frye in Oklahoma, in the warm and cosy Colwyn Bay Theatre. I always enjoyed the theatre, whether or not it was in the West End of London, or here in the provinces. Right there and then, I was in need of total peace and quiet, just so I could re-read again the script, check over my lines and become absolutely word perfect.

For Jan, who is one of my immediate neighbours, and to anyone else who claims to be uninitiated, Oklahoma is not simply a relatively flat place in the mid west of the United States of America, but it is a musical presentation by Richard Rogers and Oscar Hammerstein. Right? Understand?

The story, the nub of the musical, tells of how a girl must decide between the two suitors who both desired to take her to a social event. Laurie is just an Oklahoma farm girl who is courted by both a boisterous cowboy nicknamed Curley and by a menacing, obsessive farm hand named Jud Frye. Now, I was more than pleased as I'd been offered to play the infamous Jud. For a number of weeks, my life was congested by the mythical character, with my lines. Whether I was shopping with the family and wandering around the ubiquitous supermarket, my mind was with and in the character. If one of my family spoke to me, about those issues every ordinary family think vitally important, I'd try and mutter either a yes or no in all the right places. Once, I even went to the bathroom, forgot why I'd actually gone there in the first place, flushed the lavatory and return to my lines; then, having seen the sea ebbing and flowing, I realized how I desperately so needed the loo!

Jud's unwanted advances are rescued, in the musical, that is, by Curley who wins Laurie's hand in marriage. On the eve of their wedding day, Laurie and Curley are menaced by the drunken Jed.

'Now, we'll see how good you are as an actor, Martin,' remarked one of the more witty of stage hands, 'for you just don't drink any booze, do you?'

'I also need to die on stage and I've never done that either,' I chuckled. 'Not yet!'

Upon that rare British hot summer's day, I also wondered how many folk would turn out on such a beautiful afternoon. How many would prefer to sit through a Saturday matinee in a cosy theatre, as opposed to lying covered from top to toe in suntan lotion and sizzling on the beach? Perhaps others would prefer to come out of the heat of the day and cherish the cool of the theatre, but many already booked their tickets way in advance.

Once the matinee was through, one of the cast, along with his wife, had planned for us all to enjoy a picnic in Colwyn Bay's Eirlys Park. I had experienced their scrumptious picnics upon previous occasions. Not excluding their delicious home made pork pies, which I loved, their hampers were enough to have made any Ascot crowd drool!

Travelling to the theatre, I suddenly acquired the collywobbles. God, I thought, whatever shall I do if I forget my lines, what if I freeze to the point of not even knowing my own name, let alone my script? Straightening up to my full height, chest out, I thrust my shoulders back and told myself not to be so stupid, for this particular show wasn't my debut, my launch into the world of showbiz. No, I had performed in all sorts of British and Irish venues over the years, all with highly pleasing reviews. I had even won a number of singing competitions, along with a series of accolades in London.

On my way to Colwyn Bay, I stopped at a MacDonald's and, amidst a sea of formica table tops, I glanced over my lines. A pretty young waitress began wondering why I was taking so long with the one strawberry milkshake, to suck it up through the straw.

'Is everything all right?' she asked.

I looked up into her blue eyes. 'Perfect,' I told her with a smile.

'You want something else?'

'Nothing, thanks.'

'You could have ...'

'I'm fine.'

She told me I could please myself and she finally walked away to leave me in peace.

Backstage, I sat down before a well lit mirror; it was one of those large mirrors framed by a series of electric light bulbs, where I could see to apply my stage make-up. I cleared my throat and sang a little of: 'Lonely Room'. Prior to donning my well fitting costume and opening the various good luck cards sent to me, I tolerated the ageing joke about the roar of the grease paint and the smell of the crowd!

Finally, longing for the whole cast to know the sweet smell of success, I watched the curtain raised and hearing the audience clapping, I was on the stage! I was no longer

Martin Ward, happily living in Llandudno. No. For all and everyone, I was living and breathing Jud, deepening my character into more than just a mean bully. As Jud I was in a scene, fighting with Curley; I sensed the audience was adjusting when a distraught little girl, seated in the audience, was heard to yell out from the stalls: 'Stop it! Stop it right now, you nasty bad man, Jud, for you are hurting my daddy!' She was fearing for her father's safety and welfare.

To my distress, that wee child wasn't the only one to detach the real from the acting. The matinee over and still wearing my costume, dressed up as Jud, I was leaving by the stage door, quite alone with my innermost thoughts; I was mentally performing a post mortem upon my own performance, glad of some me time to myself, when I was aware of advancing footsteps hurrying behind me. As I quickened, so did they. Momentarily, I just glanced back and saw an elderly woman who, despite the warmth of the day, was wielding a black umbrella; at first, I thought she was a fan wanting my autograph, but then, from behind me, she thrice hit the back of my head, hard to the base of my skull, ranting and screaming at me a series of mind blowing profanities, all the time referring to me as Jud. I hunched, bringing up my shoulders in an attempt to protect myself from yet another onslaught, from the end point of that umbrella, digging into me wherever she thought fit. At one stage I struggled to get into almost a squat position. I wanted to cry out, pleading with her to stop, for how could she, such a bully, strike me another sharp blow into the middle of my shoulder blades?

'You wretch, Jud!' she shouted. 'You terrible man -.'

'What?' I considered there was no question of retaliation, not to take on this ageing aggressor, not to meet her violence with violence, but I was wondering how to control the situation when, emerging from the theatre, two of my friends came to my rescue. They saw I was in deep trouble and ran to be on the spot, they yelling at the elderly woman to clear off, to stop her hitting me. At first, they thought I was being mugged by her, but no, she really and truly believed I was Jud, needing my just desserts.

I waited for another blow, for the crazy woman was now by the side of my head. However, much to my relief, the little old lady shot one look back at the couple; suddenly, she turned away, trudging towards the town centre, way out of sight, leaving behind only the faint aroma of lavender.

I struggled to regain my composure. Damn. My head was really hurting me.

'You all right, ol' chum?' the fellow asked as his wife, an off duty A&E nurse, checked over my sore head; she was utterly convinced I should go off to Casualty, but I stated a very definite no. I was worried they'd keep me in for observation, and what about the next performance? I couldn't become a let down.

'But I believe you should go off and be checked over, Jud – whoops, I mean Martin!' she chuckled at her mistake.

'I shall be absolutely fine,' I added, although I confessed I was somewhat shaken by the whole nasty experience.

Despite all of the day's happenings, the evening show had to go on and I carried off my character without any more problems, but the attack from the little old lady's umbrella left me nursing one almighty headache. My family and the cast both agreed I was most convincing as Jud. Well, I fooled at least two, a youngster and an elderly old lady; now I really am back to being Martin in need of two paracetamol. I'm Martin and no longer Jud. Okay?

> 'The floor creaks,
> the door squeaks,
> there's a field mouse
> a – nibbling on a broom;
> And I sit here by myself,
> by myself in the lonely room.'

After the unfortunate episode with the little old lady attacking me with her umbrella, some friends began to wonder if I should tread the boards again, but, in the summer of 1962 when I was twenty-three years of age, I joined a theatrical group of entertainers based in Llandudno's Craigside Hydro Hotel.

The theatrical entertainment in which I found myself involved was variety, consisting of successive unrelated acts such as songs and dances, magic and comedy acts involving a public performance or entertainment introduced by a host known as a Master of Ceremonies. Variety all made its way from the long passed Victorian era and into regular television; such an assortment in variety shows remain popular today.

With all the rehearsals in progress, I originally applied for the post of one of the entertainers, showing myself as also a strong bass singer. The fabric of the establishment, having heard me sing, were honestly delighted to employ me and I remained with them for a few years until a dignitary personage approached me, requesting I might wish to be one of the actors in the play: "The White Sheep of the Family". The director informed me how they were looking for an Irishman to play the 'Spiv'! Well, as far as I was concerned, they need look no further; I stood before him, urging, willing him to provide me a script.

'The White Sheep of the Family' by L.du Garde Peach and Ian Hay, is an impious comedy about a family of well to do crooks who are shocked when the son, an excellent forger, quits the fold to go straight. The reason is not long hidden; he has met a girl. He takes a job in a bank (his forged references are excellent). The family makes every effort to get him back into his ancestral profession to no avail until it's discovered his fiancee is the daughter of a Scotland Yard Inspector is a first class safe breaker. The white sheep is happy to re-enter the fold and the family welcomes their talented new daughter-in-law. Half the fun of the play is the way in which the family rationalize their trade on the basis of free enterprise economics.

During my time in Artane Industrial School, one of the Christian Brothers banned me from singing as my voice, which broke early, was so strong, he telling me I would be better employed reading the English bard Shakespeare, yet in variety my deep baritone voice was gratifying and well sought after. 1997 heralded in Oliver where I was Mr Bumble and from Tuesday, 31st August to Saturday, 4th September, 1999, as part of the Llandudno Musical Players Society, I was both the Star Keeper and a baritone gentleman in the chorus of Rodgers & Hammerstein's Carousel. I cherished every moment, particularly when stealing that extra bow!

Back in the October of 1997, all my acting roles caused me to discover the Murder Mystery weekends, covering venues in Ireland, England and Wales. The occasions covered the winter season from the October to March, when hotels were struggling to fill their out of season empty rooms, opening up to otherwise known as the grisly killing games, specialising in high quality, interactive murder mystery weekends. As I tried to unearth more information, I found, first of all there was a scenario, a reason for the group of people coming together for a long weekend. Being told about it three or four weeks beforehand, I was asked to play along with all the story, with all the guests for the weekend period. However, I didn't wish to be simply one of the guests, watching and getting involved in the events which led up to the first murder and then observing the aftermath, to try to unveil the murder or murderers by the end of the weekend. No. I knew there were a number of actors who played the central roles, playing perhaps the victims, the Police Inspectors, sergeants or whoever. I took no time in applying and, with my previous track record, was snapped up by Don and Sue, the two main organisers.

I packed my bags and I was soon to be on my way to County Wicklow's Bray, the gateway to the garden of Ireland. It was early in the morning and it was icy cold. Standing in Holyhead and waiting for the Irish ferry, I could see my breath. The umpteen cars and heavy trucks out that early, left trails of vapour. Standing pink-faced in the early morning chill, having met up with Don and Sue in their vehicle, I breathed, heaving a pneumatic sigh, keen to reach the land of my birth, anxious to get to the high quality hotel in Bray, where there was waiting a warm welcome. The room would cost me nothing, for

I would be paid well for my acting abilities. It was a while since I was in Bray and I was positive I'd meet up with either some old friends or a distant relative. I half hoped I wouldn't for, once I had unpacked and ate something warm and filling, I was no longer Martin Ward, but, in character, I became Inspector Sullivan, and for the entire weekend.

Discovering as much as I could, in my acting role I was obviously as convincing as I was to the little old lady waving her umbrella, for some of the weekend guests regarded me as truly one of the Police Inspectors come out of retirement! Let me explain. During the evening meal when we dressed for dinner, folk were quite convinced I was nothing less than a high ranking officer of the law.

Apart from solving the clues to either the murder or murders, the most riveting thing about the weekend is that anything else might happen there. One evening after the main meal, a man who considered he was half way to solving the mysterious clues, entered the hotel's elevator and pressed his thumb upon the button to go up a floor. Instead, with a sudden worrying jolt, the lift plummeted into its interior mechanism, with all the sounds of whirring cogs and gears, with the sort of consequences one can only imagine. Instead of solving the murder and its series of well laid clues, the hoteliers and their electricians needed to solve their own clues as to how to extract him from the lift. Rescued, he staggered, staring and mumbling to himself while in minor shock; determined, as he was so browned off, he packed his bags and drove home.

Melancholy, another female guest, expecting too much of Inspector Sullivan, believing and mixing me up with reality, proposed marriage, offering me in return a five bedroomed house, set in its own grounds, an expensive Jaguar and a couple of Rolex wristwatches; I had to quickly explain how Inspector Sullivan might be foot loose and fancy free, but, out of character Martin Ward was a happily married man.

Over the ten years I was in character as Inspector Sullivan, I found myself pursued by guests into a real life Police Station, managing fake post mortems and acquiring pathology reports, along with folk supposing collapsing before dying in Anglesea's Buckley Arms' bar! When a real life copper came to be an unwelcome critic, he found himself handcuffed by me until he promised not to spoil the fun of being a sleuth!

My years of singing and acting caused me to discover how in the year of 2008 Tudno FM were hunting for radio presenters; discussed at length in chapter ten, I couldn't not apply, now could I?

# CHAPTER TWELVE

# "PAINTING A PICTURE IN WORDS"

Any nervousness I may well have experienced simply fell away and I offered one of my beaming broad smiles.

'Ah, so then, Martin, you've decided to join with us, after all?' quizzed the coordinator, returning my smile and sitting herself back into her chair; I could hear a faint buzzing, not unlike the sound of an escaped wasp, yet it wasn't any such stinging bug. I realised she was seated in one of those smart office chairs where, at the press of a red button, it gave her lower back a gentle massage. Fleetingly, secretly, I wondered if I would be provided with a similar such piece of equipment. There was nothing at all the matter with my back, and any of my lumbar muscles felt in tip-top condition but, coming to work there, I simply fancied a go in such a multi-purpose swivel chair!

She told me: 'That's unbelievably good news for all of us here.'

My mind wandered only for a brief moment. What was the good news?

'Yes indeed, Martin, it will be special to have you on our team.'

Oh, that. I confess I am usually a fairly quiet, shy man until I actually come to know the individual person or persons; it's then when I find no cat has my tongue, relax and chat on nineteen to the dozen, yet always in the nicest way possible, always trying to entertain, attempting to enthral my listener. Having my early retirement looming up before me, I was contemplating, wondering, in fact, what I'd actually do with all those golden years stretching out before me. I didn't want to be one of those sat in front of the 'goggle box' day in, day out. I reckon my highly active mind would go into scrambled eggs and not those consumed on toast! Oh, sure, I enjoy viewing the television as much as the next, but only in very small doses. Almost usually only seeing the BBC News, the weather forecast and the occasional film, perhaps in black and white, is quite enough. I also love our immediate family; they live quite nearby, yet, all settled now with families of their own, I do not think I should be living in their pockets, however welcoming they are. There were already odd moments of time when I was already getting bored, especially on a Friday, although what was wrong with Fridays? Perhaps it was all to do with the soaps? Unlike my spouse, I wasn't at all interested in them; I still feel precisely the same.

My wife and I were, for a while, involved in various aspects of the theatre, especially travelling to many locations, far and wide, to be part of whodunit 'murder' weekends. It was spotted how, during my time on the stage, treading the boards, as it were, I have a good, clear voice. I would invariably be called back for a bravo encore, several times to take a bow.

Some powers that be informed me: 'Even though you can be a quiet gentleman, a softly spoken Irishman, your diction is especially good for radio work.' As a result, the coordinator for 'Talking books for the Blind' and the 'Talking Newspapers' discovered such accolades and roped me in to read, to also tell some of my imaginary tales. 'We absolutely adore all your stories,' she said, 'and so shall the two hundred plus blind folk … they'll find them magical!'

My bright green eyes widened and my mind suddenly went into an overdrive. Two hundred people? Had I heard her quite correctly? She stated there'd maybe even more? And all over Conwy and beyond? Was she in the buzzing chair totally serious for it's no small area? Frankly, I thought I'd be in either in a community hall or in the lounge of a nursing home, sitting perhaps all in a semi-circle, chatting with a few partially sighted old folk – not quite so many. Ah, well, I thought, in for a penny, in for a pound … here goes … it was either that, or taking up making bread again with its fabulous aroma. Oh, I know there's nothing much to compare with the smell of freshly baked Irish soda bread, unless it's sizzling bacon first thing on a Sunday morning – bacon and eggs with freshly baked bread; ooh, it's probably my idea of heaven upon earth!

However, I digress!

I wondered what type of stories I should tell over the airwaves to those blind and partially sighted. I knew the one about the actress and the Bishop, but maybe not! No, definitely not such a one, and, anyway, it's more of a crazy and ancient old joke rather than a good story, so perhaps I needed to start being a little more sensible, me thinks.

During one of my imaginary stories I told of an old granddad who lived in the Urals. I knew about the Urals from a geography lesson given when I was a young school boy; I knew they were a mountainous range in western Russia. Well, one Sunday morning, over the airwaves on my radio show I told of an old fellow, a Russian granddad who skidded and sat down hard on the ice, somehow he becoming stuck into it. I added how his beloved family would come and attend to his personal and private needs, feeding him with hearty beef stews, shaving his chin and so on. Some of them would even bring out a plaid blanket and enjoy a pleasant picnic with the old guy. They cared for him exceedingly well until the summer sun began to melt the ice, when his well built posterior was finally freed. The following days some listeners contacted me, worried sick about the old Russian, how he would surely have died from hypothermia. I cracked up laughing and needed the next Sunday to broadcast a confession that I made it all up; there was no such granddad with his fat rear stuck into the ice! One Dubliner, now living in Colwyn Bay, was so relieved it was a lot of fiction, simply as she was about a scientist who had a cabin in the rain forest; he couldn't get out because of the rain! Eventually, I told lots of tales, but one of my favourites was of a man who I shall simply name as Tom. Are you also ready to know all about him? Well, here we go; sit yourself down in a really comfy old armchair with a nice cup of tea and I shall tell you much about him.

Old Tom lived in Tyn-y-coed. The house was named Tyn-y-coed, for translating it from Welsh into the English, means: 'House in the Trees'. And that's simply what it was - an old farmhouse nestling among some tall trees.

Ooh, I like trees, especially Horse Chestnut trees. I once said, but only in jest, if I were a tree, I should love to be a Horse Chestnut tree, all full of conkers where young kids could be playing, yet here I go again, for I should keep my mind from wandering from the matter in hand. I only wondered if any of you had conker fights when you were young? I certainly did and I bet old Tom did, too. I am sure, when Tom was only a little guy, he'd have threaded a length of string through the middle of a large, shiny brown conker and he'd see if he could use it to beat his opponent, smashing his one into smithereens. Although only happening once a year, it's great fun and I think I'd even enjoy it now, given half a chance!

In defence of men never growing up, French writer Francoise Sagan once said: 'I like a man to really act like a man … strong and childish.' I reckon she'd have liked me very much!

During the First World War, the rambling old farmhouse in question, was then requisitioned as a convalescent home, but really to only be used for some ageing army Captains and and old Majors. However, for many years Tom had worked in Tyn-y-coed and, as a result, he'd been provided with a nice two-bedroomed apartment. During those far off times, that same attic dwelling went with his job, as it were. I suppose his nice little home was then regarded in the self same way as a tithe cottage. His landlord, a helpful soul, stated how retired Thomas, he nearly always known simply as 'Tom', could see out his days up there; it was planned how he'd be rent free, but Tom had his pride, so he paid only a nominal amount. He was indeed comfortable up in the apartment.

Something had most definitely woken Tom. He usually slept like the proverbial log, but not on that particular night; he was well and truly awake. Phew! It was a most odd feeling; he pricked up his ears to try and listen, yet everywhere was so hushed you could have virtually heard a pin drop ... that is, if you had a pin to drop!

Strange, he thought. How odd it all feels around me.

The elderly fellow pulled himself up, propping himself upon one elbow and reached for his bi-focal spectacles; using the edge of his sheet, he cleaned the lenses before popping them on and, running his long fingers through his thinning, but tousled white hair, he squinted to look at his bedside alarm clock. Ten to two in the early hours of the morning? No. Was that all it was? He thought it surely had to be later than ten to two, yet it really wasn't. His weakened heart also felt as if it was racing nineteen to the dozen, within his chest wall and up into the left side of his neck. He'd been previously diagnosed with a bit of angina, in the past, but, as far as he could remember, nothing felt quite as weird as this. He decided he would get up and make himself a nice cup of tea; someone once informed him how a cup of tea was the cure for all ills, although it actually isn't! Yes, that's it; he'd boil the electric kettle and make himself a strong brew in his favourite mug, into the beaker which had 'Tom' printed on one side. He was given it with a milk chocolate egg a few Easters before. He'd felt like a big kid when he received it from a young friend, yet it was a bit of fun to smash the egg. He shared the chocolate around as too much of it gave him a rotten headache. Cheese and red wine invariably did the same so there was no point in having to spoil his time unnecessarily.

Tom was still at a loss as to know that which woke him at precisely ten to two; he was still wondering when it was if the solution hit him bang between the eyes. He realized it must have been the sheer sound of silence. It seemed somewhat odd to say so, but, as he parted his curtains aside, he stared out and saw the snow, silently falling like umpteen feathers in an unusual formation. So hushed, yet maybe it was that which roused him and he simply smiled to himself, for how could the intense quiet have disturbed his sleep? If there'd been a loud hullabaloo he could have understood, but how could a silence wake him? Whatever, it definitely seemed that way.

He'd resided in the same house for more years than he cared to remember, only living up in that self same apartment, his little attic with its compact fitted kitchen and smart, well equip bathroom. His wife Kathrine also lived there once, yet she'd died peacefully in her sleep one beautiful summer's night. They'd both regretted never having any children of their own, but they cherished their love, with their photographic memories.

Tyn-y-coed in which Tom lived had changed ownership several times and now, down below, on the ground floor were solicitors' offices; perhaps, he wondered, when they left for home, the last employee to leave forgot to turn off their lights. Tom possessed a master key and he could have nipped down to switch off their lights, yet he didn't; for some reason he changed his mind for the only light within his vision somewhat puzzled him and it just wouldn't turn off. The light wasn't seemingly quite normal – it was more of a frosty opaque, rather than the usual transparent; he squinted yet he still couldn't quite see through it until … until he noticed the big armchairs - two of them. They were somehow familiar to him.

He cleared some huskiness in his throat with a bit of a cough and shielded his eyes with one hand over his brows, in the way one does during strong sunlight.

'Hello, who is it?' he questioned. 'Who's there? Come on out now and speak up whoever you are!'

'Ah, you don't know me quite yet, but, Tom, I most certainly do know you,' came the enigmatic reply.

Tom adjusted his spectacles, pushing the bridge of them up his nose and gulped hard – to put it mildly, he was totally aghast. On and off, he'd lived up in the attic for at least fifty-five years; nothing like this had ever happened to him before. Not ever.

'Do you remember when you first came, when you and your brother went scrumping for apples, pinching carrots and pulling up potatoes?'

He did.

'Apart from the meat, your mammy had virtually everything for a hearty Sunday roast lunch!'

Yes, of course, naturally Tom did indeed remember, but he and his brother Harry weren't wanting to become bad lads; they only planned to take enough pieces of fruit and vegetables so not to be noticed by the head gardener.

'Even so, you'd heard: "I'll get him!" and you thought the Matron-in-charge had uncovered your misdemeanors, had discovered your scrumping.'

Tom did.

There was a chuckle in the voice. 'Hey, she wasn't after you at all, but she was seeking out her little Jack Russell dog ... that was all!'

'What?'

'Do you remember all those long ago times, Tom?'

Oh, yes, Tom well remembered all right - all those far off days of yesteryear. He actually remembered those days way better than in the present; he kept a day-to-day diary for this present year, yet, despite all, he could recollect the days of his youth so very well indeed. Tom remembered when he'd once taken a whole sack of ripe red apples; when he was very nearly caught, he threw it over some privet hedging so not to be discovered. Phew! It was a very long time ago when all this happened.

'Are you feeling all right, Tom?'

Tom was suddenly feeling grand, really grand; he twitched his muscles and his osteoarthritis hadn't been so pain free for donkey's years. Frankly, he was quite delighted.

Covering his pyjama bottoms with his silky dressing gown and slipping his bare feet into his old, comfy slippers, slowly, carefully, Tom wandered through a big creaky old door, a door which led right down into the basement where the once steam filled kitchens were originally situated, when there were once thirty patients, when they all sat around chatting together in a large lounge. Strange. It was also becoming to Tom not unlike yesterday, too. There was the retired army Major in his fine regimental dress uniform, someone who he hadn't seen for simply ages, not since he, Tom, was knee high to a grasshopper.

'Oh, Tom, I haven't seen you since you were a nipper, when you were no more than about five or six years of age. Gosh, how you've grown!' remarked Mr Horn. In those distant days he was then the Head Waiter of yesteryear; he always looked very smart in his pristine grey pinstriped trousers and black tailed coat.

There was both he and the Major standing to attention before him, almost as large as life. He looked around. Where on earth, he wondered, had they come from?

Tom turned around and, hey-ho, there was his Kathrine, the girl he'd married, who'd left him with a gut-wrenching emptiness in his evenings, in his nights, yet quite suddenly, he could gently feel the touch of her soft hand. He remembered those cherished moments when they'd sit together, when he'd take her hand in his and she would so welcome the warmth of his skin, wishing he'd held her more often; why didn't she tell him so, yet perhaps she was a little shy, too? Maybe she considered he should be the one to always make the first move, otherwise he might have thought her being brash, too forward; she was never quite sure. What she did know, she loved him so very much; oh, she wished they'd never been separated, too.

Whoever was talking to him, whoever was doing his best to comfort him, declared: 'Come on, Tom, and let me show you around, only a little more.'

Tom felt he should be scared stiff, yet he wasn't a bit worried, not at all bothered when he saw the royal blue uniform of the Matron-in-charge; her greying hair, plaited into a coronet, was half covered by a frilly lace cap. She glanced down at her silver fob watch. It was also showing ten to two. Upright, too, she was walking in with a big beaming smile; she took Tom by the hand, leading him outside where there were the green, green lawns, where there were those residents all still playing croquet. 'I always knew it was you who was scrumping apples, Thomas!' She chuckled, but then the tone of her voice changed to that of one with a deep warmth, a caring in the way he was spoken to; she was basically such a kind person, a people person.

As Tom stroked the previous day's stubble sprouting on his chin, he thought, remembering when he was about twenty-one and, then the coming of age, it was then his special birthday. As he looked, passing by his unusually odd, opaque light, he saw some folk on bikes, all ready to go off for an outing; there were so few motorcars ... only one or two black Fords and Austin Sevens – not a bit like today with the fast four lane motorways.

The comforting voice behind the strange opaque light led Tom to climb the carpeted flights of stairs back to his attic home, yet, unusually, he was walking with a spring in his step, as if he was still a youngster, as if it was remaining a yesteryear. Where was the coming day? Whatever would happen to it? he wondered.

'Well, Tom, old chap, would you like to come with me, to see all your special friends, or to stay put in this House of Trees?' asked the aged Army Major. 'What do you think concerning that, my chum, eh?'

Tom gulped and slightly hesitated for he was the teeniest bit unsure, yet only for the very shortest of whiles. Tired through and through, he settled back with a long pneumatic sigh and gently fell fast asleep; the elderly fellow hadn't climbed back into his nice warm bed, but into his favourite comfy armchair, up in the attic apartment where he'd lived for many contented years. At total peace now, Tom's final words were: 'I'm here to stay, here, where I feel grand, where I am most happy - in Tyn-y-coed.'

The Health Centre's on call General Practitioner was called out to check him over, yet, sadly, she confirmed the gentle old man had died from natural causes, a little like those of his beloved Kathrine; the time of Tom's death was presumed to be at ten to two. The very odd thing was how nobody noticed his three time clocks; the one upon the wall, the one on the mantle-piece and the third being by his bedside had all stopped exactly at ten to two. Strange? Whatever, yet really, to both you and me, we know full well Tom had simply stopped where everyone of his memories remained.

\* \* \*

## "PIDDLING PETE"

A famous dog came once to town
whose middle name was Pete.
His pedigree was two yards long,
his looks were hard to beat.

And as he trotted down the road,
'twas beautiful to see,
his work on every corner,
his work on every tree.

He watered every gateway,
he never missed a post.
For piddling was his masterpiece
and piddling was his boast.

The city dogs stood looking on
with deep and jealous rage,
to see this simple country dog,
the piddler of his age,

They smelled him over one by one,
they smelled him two by two,
the noble Pete in high distain
stood still till they were through.

163

They sniffed him over one by one
their praise for him ran high,
but when one sniffed him underneath,
Pete piddled in his eye.

Then just to show the city dogs
he didn't care a damn,
Pete strolled into a grocer's shop
and piddled on a ham!

He piddled on his onions,
he piddled on the floor,
And when the grocer kicked him out,
he piddled on the door.

Behind him all the city dogs
debated what to do,
they'd hold a piddling carnival
to show this stranger through.

They showed him all the piddling posts
they knew around the town,
they started out with many winks
to wear the stranger down.

But Pete was with their every trick
with vigour and with vim;
A thousand piddles more or less
were all the same to him ...

And on and on went noble Pete
his hind leg kicking high.
While most were lifting legs in bluff
or piddling mighty dry.

And on and on went noble Pete,
watering every dale and hill,
'till each and every city dog
was piddled to a standstill.

Then Pete and exhibition gave
of all the ways to piddle,
Like, double drips and fancy flips,
and now and then a dribble.

And all the while the city dogs
did neither wink or grin,
Pete blithely piddled out of town
as he had piddled in.

The city dogs said: "So long, Pete,
your piddling did defeat us!"
But no-one ever put them wise
that Pete had diabetes.

(Anon)

✻ ✻ ✻

# 'THE LAST CREAM DOUGHNUT'

## A SHORT STORY
## BY MARTIN P A WARD

It was known as a lazy wind, for it didn't go around the person, but seemed to pierce straight through.

'Don't you dare go out without your thick wool scarf, George. Do you hear me?'

The old guy heard all right. For a split second he paused and, raising his grey-green eyes heavenwards, he half smiled, making off in the direction of the newsagent. Every Thursday, without fail, it had long become George Jones' habit to pick up his wife's Daily Post, along with his own North Wales' Weekly News.

With only a few days prior to Christmas morning, Freddie, the newsagent, offered the old chap seasonal greetings. George, as always, placed the correct number of coins, one after the other across the counter and thanked him before politely returning the same felicitations. Freddie couldn't remember many Thursdays when the now eighty-two year old didn't trail the two-hundred yards to collect the newspapers.

'Bethan all right, is she, George? I heard she's got a bit of arthritis. That right, is it?'

'Aye, she's not too bad, although this damp weather doesn't help much.' Inwardly, he knew her weight didn't help her joints, but it was more than his life was worth to add a comment about what he spied on the bathroom scales!

'And what are you doing for Christmas? The usual?'

As always, George and Bethan Jones visited their only daughter Sally and son-in-law; they, too, lived in the historical coastal town of Llandudno. Every Christmas it became George's job to make the onion gravy; his son-in-law invariably remarked how George made a better job of the onion sauce than did Sally, yet she showed no offence. Sally, now approaching those middle years, was their only child. They'd have secretly liked more kids, but it never seemed to happen, just as their being grandparents hadn't. He naturally did wonder about such issues, yet he was of a generation when men were men and excluded from the whispers of 'women's stuff'.

With the two newspapers folded and tucked under his arm, his gloved hands stuffed deep into his winter coat's pockets, George glanced up at the overcast sky with its advancing grey clouds; he wondered, becoming suspicious if the bookmakers were right, betting odds on how there'd be a white Christmas. He was pleased to soon be back indoors. Unwinding his long green scarf and leaving it with his coat on a hook in the hall, he was more than ready for a thumping good breakfast. Rubbing his hands together, he made it straight through to the kitchen where Bethan, his wife, was making breakfast. She was happy enough with a plate of cereal and toast, but he fancied something more substantial, something more warming in his empty stomach.

'You want some porridge, George?' she asked. 'Toast, too?'

He preferred his three thick slices of hot buttered toast well-done, but, after nearly sixty-three years of marriage, Bethan knew all of his foibles, his idiosyncrasies. Even so, through their golden years, they'd sold up their large family home and settled into a small comfy apartment in Llandudno, near its Oval.

George and Bethan had an unspoken house rule that whoever cooked, didn't wash the dishes; with the breakfast items cleared away, they parked themselves in the living room, feet up and relaxing against some cushions. She reminded how the doctor advised him not to cross his ankles, but, exaggerating a loud sigh, he did it anyway to be comfortable! It was their want to settle down to read the newspapers. Setting his aside, George invariably left his edition until the evening when, to the easy listening of the local radio, he'd do his utmost to complete the quick crossword; he cherished those quieter moments, away from the various soaps blaring out on TV. She'd become quite a television-addict, but, apart from the News and the occasional film, George stated he could well do without the large contraption.

It was during that particular Thursday morning how George read out the headlines, declaring how one of the town's officials would be up before the beak for corruption, a former councillor was to receive a jail sentence and his long standing secretary-cum-mistress was getting five years for a similar offence. The presiding judge stated it was a gross breach of Conwy's public trust.

Bethan did not seem overly shocked, but simply stated: 'Fancy that. Let's go out, eh, George?'

'Are you really sure? It's jolly cold out there.'

'I know, but I don't want to stay inside. Not today.'

Wrapping up warm with extra layers of thick winter clothing, they arm in arm, aimed for the local reference library.

The old couple turned right upon the corner of Lloyd and Mostyn Streets, making towards the library building, approximately two hundred yards.

Bethan Jones commented upon the radical changes in Lloyd Street. 'I swear it never use to be this busy years ago. Now, when I was still in my twenties - .'

'Aye, but you're thinking ... what, sixty or seventy years ago?' George interrupted, slowing up to catch his breath, breath he could see like smoke escaping in the cold.

She indicated towards one of the street corners. 'Remember, George, it use to be a butcher's shop? I used to buy us some lovely cuts of Welsh lamb from there. Oh, he's long gone, and so has the co-op where we got our dividends.'

George remarked how the co-op was now a fish and chip shop.

'I can still remember the grocer's, but I cannot think for the life in me what he was called ...'

He gave her arm a little squeeze.'Oh, you can! It's name was "Mason's" and I reckon old man Mason's saucy assistant was quite sweet on you. Yes, come to think about it, that Harry fellow fancied you something rotten! He'd have married you, given half the chance.'

'Ooh, George, stop it!' Bethan had turned eighty, but she gave a silly giggle, not unlike a young lass might become coy.

In the main street there was much movement from busy traffic, along with equally bustling people, last minute Christmas shoppers, several of whom the pair was positive they knew, for they'd resided in Llandudno for more years than they cared to remember. Traffic cops and wardens were out in force. Near to one of the Marks and Spencers' stores the Salvation Army band was playing as ever: 'God rest ye merry gentlemen' and 'Joy to the world' before rattling their money tins under the shoppers' noses for their collections.

'It'll be a darn sight warmer inside, out of this biting wind.' George looked up again at the sky with its heavily laden clouds. 'I reckon we're in for a snow fall ... let's get inside, Bethan, before we freeze to blooming death.'

In the Library's entrance were long stretches of artworks, framed and still ready for sale. There were other displays under glass which managed to be unfortunately scribed in ancient Greek, to which George wittingly stated it was 'all Greek' to him! The pair made for the elevator rather than the flight of stairs; Bethan complained the arthritis in her poor old knees would have been an issue. Upon the first floor Mrs Evans who was the chief librarian, glanced up at the familiar Jones', kindly greeting them with a welcoming smile before leading them to their familiar spot ... a table directly under the Georgian style window. 'You both look as if you have cold faces.' They had and the old guy's nose was red with the chill. The librarian leaned forward, asking if they'd each fancy a mug of tea. They did indeed. Long gone were the days when loose leaf tea brewed in a warmed pot; now there were either triangular or round teabags in a mug, yet it would still warm the cockles of their hearts.

Fleetingly, Bethan craned her neck to stare out, yet, with nothing riveting to see, she chose to read a little of a Maeve Binchy biography, yet George Jones' mind was engrossed in someone or other's memoirs concerning the Korean War, a war starting in June, 1950 and continuing for three long years.

A captivating youngish fellow, probably in his early thirties, for it was difficult to tell, was quietly moving across the library floor, nearing to where the Jones' sat. He noticed the vacant seat at their table. 'Do you mind if I sit here, or would I be disturbing you?' he asked.

George cared not. Bethan didn't see it as an encroachment and half welcomed the distraction, she always keen for some added and chatty company. 'It's warmer in here, isn't it?' she remarked.

Outside the tourists, the overloaded cars full of Christmas fare moved bumper to bumper while gulls danced and reeled. The stranger at their table had enough of the 'silly season' and required space and time to glance over his lines. 'I'm an actor, you see,' he stated. He had been in a whole series of theatrical performances, yet he would soon be playing the lead role in the local theatre. 'My real name is Cornelius Lane. How do you do?'

Impressed by meeting a real live actor, in a state of amazement, Bethan told Cornelius she was thrilled to bits to meet him, asking if he called everyone 'lovey', to which he shook his head and laughed. Whatever, she was pleased to meet him; George remained nonplussed until she nudged him. 'We wish Cornelius well, don't we, dear?'

'Yes, son. So, what are you ... what's your part?'

'I was saying to your wife how I am playing the lead role ... in "The picture of Dorian Gray". Oscar Wilde wrote it, you know.'

The old man didn't know. He had never heard of the play.

'It's being shown here in the New Year.' He added how it was the story of one beautiful, innocent young man's seduction, moral corruption and eventual downfall.

'Really? My wife and I use to enjoy the occasional night out at the theatre.'

'In that case, I could get you a couple of free theatre tickets, if you so wish?'

'You sure about that?'

He was. Totally sure and it would be his pleasure.

Excluding the young actor from their conversation, George glanced up at a wall clock, comparing it with his own wristwatch, realising it to be lunchtime.

Bethan picked up on upon his rumbling tummy. 'George, dear, where should we go for lunch today? The Imperial Hotel?'

He exhaled a long pneumatic sigh, adding how they'd already eaten at the Imperial Hotel. 'We ate there yesterday.' He persisted how they dined during the previous Tuesday in the Meirion Hotel. 'What about having luncheon, by walking up to the top of town and see if we can get a reservation in the Empire Hotel?' He knew she enjoyed their warming chicken soup, with a bread roll; it was also well known for their large cream doughnuts. 'You're really fond of those, aren't you, Bethan?'

She chuckled, asking what he'd have.

He bit his bottom lip and thought, wondering if he might have a tasty chicken sandwich, followed by a Waldorf salad. 'I reckon I fancy a rum and raisin ice-cream, too. Yeah, that's what I shall have.'

'Brr, bit too cold for ice-cream, after all, it's December, George.'

The old guy gave a shrug. 'Perhaps, but it is what I fancy and a little of what you fancy does you good, eh?'

Pausing, Bethan frowned; suddenly her mind flicked back to the time when they first encountered one and another. 'Tell me, George, dear, do you remember our very first meeting?'

'Oh, sweet lady, you know full well I do.'

'Tell me then exactly what you remember ...'

George Jones shook his head, cleaned his spectacles and smiled, remembering the third day of September way back in 1939. He was in a local bakery, purchasing two fresh cream doughnuts when the confectioner declared they were the very last ones ... there were no more doughnuts remaining. 'Seeing them, I decided to buy them when I heard a sweet young voice asking for a cream doughnut. "Sorry, lass, but that young fellow who is leaving, bought the very last two and I shall not be making any more doughnuts, not with war probably about to break out." Before any more could be said, the baker's radio ceased its incessant music to hear Neville Chamberlain, the then Prime Minister state just the prediction ...'

Oh, Bethan well remembered that historical moment, when it was sadly announced Britain was at war with Germany. No-one knew how to react, yet customers still had to be served. 'Carry on, George, and keep talking, for I love to hear you tell the tale.'

He sighed, but did as she asked, only to please her.

As he vacated the bakery, he waited to find out if a then young Bethan might share his cream doughnuts. 'It was then a lovely sunny day and I thought we could both nip down to the beach.'

'We did.'

'Aye. The two of us sat on a seat for two, in a shelter, watching the far off boats – there a regatta ... remember? The sea was so very calm and blue.'

Bethan leaned forward and chuckled a little too loudly before noticing a library sign, stating: "Silence, please". She reminisced with a fondness how George had asked her to choose one of the buns. Her big brown eyes lit up as she naughtily picked the larger; taking a huge, greedy bite, it left a white 'moustache' of cream and upon the tip of her nose. She knew in her heart of hearts, she and George would marry. 'There was no-one else for me, you know? Never.'

'No regrets?'

'Oh, no. We were young then, and here we are, in our eighties, still in love -.'

Cornelius, the youngish actor, had overheard the Jones' reminiscing. He was not a little confused when Bethan declared: 'That was a scrumptious lunch today, George.'

'It was indeed.'

'Did you enjoy your ice-cream?'

He smiled, but Cornelius became perplexed. Deciding enough was enough, he quietly remarked to the librarian, it was time to go home. 'Before I do, please, are you able to tell me … who are the odd couple by the window?'

Mrs Evans smiled. 'Why do you ask?'

'Being near to them, it was somewhat hard to concentrate.'

'Sorry about that but …'

Cornelius wasn't being critical, yet his mind seemed in a turmoil, for the old couple did seem a bizarre.

Mrs Evans explained they liked to think about all their yesterdays, about the time they met, dreaming where they might have been for lunch, and so on. Nothing more.

'But they never left their seats!' he exclaimed. 'They never left the library to eat any lunch.'

Later, prior to the Jones' leaving for home, Bethan reminded George to wrap his scarf well round his neck, to which he asked: 'What the Dickens do you think I am going to do with the thing, huh?' It was then the librarian called after them, for them to wait. The old couple both stared back, wondering what was the matter.

'Remember the young guy at your table? He hurriedly returned with a box; it's been left for you two. It has to be for you as it says it's for the old couple at the table by the window.'

'Why didn't he give it to us in person, then?' Bethan asked.

No-one knew, but inside the box were two theatre tickets, along with two large, and I mean large cream doughnuts, yet one slightly bigger than the other. George and Bethan, along with Mrs Evans were not simply astounded, for their eyes widened in amazement.

'I know the one Bethan will have,' laughed George, 'and she'll end up with a white cream moustache!'

'Merry Christmas to you both!'

'Thank you, Mrs Evans ...and to the Cornelius Lanes wherever and whoever you are.'

* * *

# The Contract

## A Short Story
## by Martin P A Ward

The previous day the skies were blue and the air was as crisp as celery. Only the higher ground was snow capped. However, the evening became a whole new ball game. Snow flakes began to fly, flinging themselves first into a brown sludge until visibility became a no, no. Anyone with a modicum of sense, abandoned their vehicles, returned home and simply looked out of their windows at the most incredibly white beauty of the creation. Mr Nicolas De-ville was a man upon a mission. He had little choice but to keep plodding on through the bleak weather where snow was swirling, fluffy and benign. Roads were becoming a curse, featureless and seemingly endless, with vanishing points as if one may venture nowhere. Trudging three feet more, his legs were aching, they half felt as if they were belonging to someone else. Finding himself walking down the centre of the County Road, it was becoming as dark as pitch. He was well wrapped up against the elements, but the snow, the Arctic-type flakes, were even landing upon his bushy brows, along with his eyelashes, too, causing difficulty in his seeing. With eight feet hedges on his either side, he knew he was still on track. For a split second or two, he turned to see from whence he came, yet it was too dark to see his footprints; if he had noticed them, they'd already have been covered by fresh snow. To be sure, it was a tough night to be out and about. He'd been a couple of times before, but not for many years. He seemed to remember how ahead there was an amber coloured street lamp; it was upon the crossroads and on the lower ground towards Beddington's arable and livestock farm. The nearer he came to it, the brighter it naturally became and he could just about spot a lamplight in the porch way, over the far door to his destination. There were three large detached houses, all well spaced. The first house belonged to a well-heeled surgeon, she specialising in plastic surgery. Another home belonged to an actor who claimed he was 'resting' in between parts. The third one was owned by Michael and Rosie Sullivan; Michael was always known as Mike to his friends and associates.

Mike was a successful businessman who, some years previously, purchased the Beddington Farmstead, consisting of fifty acres and a pretty cottage which he, with the help of his two older sons, renovated. Rosie loved it so much she and Mike moved in, leaving the rest of the acreage for a local farmer to rent. Everything for the Sullivan couple was ideal; childhood sweethearts, they were well-suited for each other. They knew it, too, and so did all those romantics known to them.

As Mr De-ville finally made it up the few steps to the Sullivan's home, Mike and Rosie had said their good-nights to their neighbours, folk who'd visited them for a warming late supper-type meal.

'Are you all right, Mike?' asked their surgeon friend's other half. 'I've never known you so quiet!'

'It's nothing. I'm fine.'

'You're not sickening for that 'flu, are you? There's a lot of it about, you know.'

Rosie pushed in and felt Mike's forehead with the back of her hand. 'Are you all right, darling?'

He shrugged it all off as fussing, as foolish nonsense, reassuring everyone how he really was okay.

When all their neighbours left, Mike briefly glanced at himself in a nearby hall mirror. He stroked his neatly refined greying beard; perhaps he did look washed out, but he knew it was probably because he was waiting for yet another visitor; he told Rosie someone else was coming at around 11.45 pm., and no ordinary fellow, at that, although he didn't let on to her how it'd be a slight oddball. She would worry herself.

Rosie glanced at her wristwatch before frowning at him. 'Mike, it's a bit late to be having even more visitors …'

'Sorry, pet. It is to be a late night business meeting, and one I cannot wriggle from …'

'But it is so late, and it's a hazardous night to be out. You're not going out there, are you?'

'I know it's late and I am hoping I shall not need to go out anywhere. The meeting simply cannot be avoided.'

'At least our guests this evening only had to go nearby, but, this man … who on earth is he?'

'Stop concerning yourself. You go on up to bed.'

Rosie put a hand to her mouth and yawned. 'I must admit I am feeling tired. It's been a busy evening.'

With the kitchen left tidy and the dishwasher loaded, she'd just made it to bed when there came a rapping upon their front door. Under the light of the porch stood a man, his gloved hand outstretched.

'Come on inside and leave your coat and boots in the hall. Forgive me if I do not shake you hand.' Anxiously, Mike stated: 'You'd better come through into my study.'

Mike's study was redesigned along the lines of a smart London's 'gentlemen's club' ; he'd once attended such a place in Westminster. He was with his father-in-law who was a member of such a haunt. With such ideas swirling around in his head, he purchased a knee-holed antique desk upon which stood a silver framed photograph, along with a small green lamp, a light more for atmosphere than use. His ultimate pride and joy were a couple of deep brown leather, high backed Chesterfields; one of the sumptuous chairs came with a matching swivelled footstool; three of the walls were mostly lined with the classics, books he always planned to read, yet hadn't.

Mr De-ville spied the half full crystal decanters. 'I could do with a brandy, to warm the cockles of my heart, Michael.'

'Please yourself. It is quite late, so I'd prefer you came straight to the point, Mr De-ville.'

'Fair enough. I hope you have made all your arrangements for your departure, to have said all your goodbyes to family and friends.'

Mike's brow knitted together. 'Mr De-ville, I am begging you, please, please, may we come to another arrangement?'

'Not a cat in hell's chance!' The old guy shook his head, fishing out a copy of the agreement from a pocket which he waved under Mike's nose. 'You planned to sell your soul for money ... you signed an official contract with me. See?'

'I know, when we signed the contract, all those years ago, I was then only a young man. I was trying to provide for my family but it was hard. I was in desperate need of ready cash.'

'And you made the flippant remark how you would sell your soul for some money.'

Mike placed his elbows on his knees, his head in his hands. He looked up under hooded eyelids, up into the old man's harsh, dark eyes. 'I didn't really mean what I said, about selling my soul …'

'Ah, but that'll teach you to watch what you say! Anyway, remember that I gave you those eight numbers and told you to do the Pools; that Saturday night, all those years ago, the numbers came up - £2.9 million pounds!'

'And, heavens! I was the only winner.'

'Don't mentioned heaven! I do not like it.' Mr De-ville promptly changed the subject to ask: 'And, did you actually need all that money? So, answer me.'

Mike shook his head, stating how he only required £500,000 to set his business on its feet.'

'Yes, and there you were with £2,400,000 remaining, enough to multiply your business five fold.'

Mike knew Mr De-ville desired to snatch it all from him. 'You need to give it all to me, Michael, my man. Every last penny must be all mine.'

'No!'

'Oh, but yes! You see, we had a binding contract, written partly in your own life's blood!' Mr De-ville rubbed his ageing hands together and chuckled. 'I have fulfilled my part of it – now you must keep your part of the arrangement. Right?'

Mike wasn't agreeable. He thought of his lovely Rosie tucked down and quietly sleeping upstairs, totally oblivious to his late night guest, that nasty old man. There was the person who he'd hoped upon hope he'd never see again; he hadn't wished to set eyes upon that wretched contract, let alone Mr De-ville. Surely, there had to be a way out, a part which perhaps he overlooked, yet it was a long shot. He wondered if he would ever be free. His thoughts of freedom were sharply interrupted by the old chap declaring: 'This contract stated how I would arrive at your home, not a minute before, not a second after 11.45 pm on the last day of February. You and I shall leave according to the contract, one minute after twelve midnight on the 28th February. So, then, Michael Sullivan, let's go; you have a date with the inferno. Where you are going, you won't need your winter coat. Let's now be off!'

The old clock on the mantle piece began to ring out twelve steady chimes. On the last chime, Mike's blue eyes began to glisten with a laughter in a manically way. He threw his head back and laughed until he almost cried tears.

The old person was stuporous, as if helplessly amazed. What's the lunatic laughing at, he wondered.

'I'll tell you, Mr De-ville! Look, look at that clock on my mantle piece .'

'Yeah, so what about it?'

'Well, it shows not only the time but the date, too. See?'

De-ville took his socked feet from the footstool; he rose from his chair and stared at the old timepiece which showed the date to be the 28th of February. 'Aye,' he declared, 'it is the final day of the month. So, come on, Sullivan, for your soul belongs to me now ...'

Mike shook his head. 'You and I had a contract only for the last day of the month, yet it isn't – tomorrow is the last day ... the 29th is the final day!'

Mr De-ville scratched his head. 'How come?'

'I'll tell you. This year is a leap year, the only time when a woman may officially propose marriage to the man with whom she is in love.

'Are you lying to me, Sullivan?'

'Not at all. This year is a leap year with the 29th being the final day of February, so, you, Mr Nick De-ville, you are the one who has broken the contract by coming here one day too soon. Therefore, I am free! I am free from you ... you and your wretched contract!'

The old devil, the old Nick who went by the ungracious pseudonym of Mr Nick De-ville wasn't slow in demonstrating his miserable and low state of disappointment; he rapidly returned back to the dark, snowy wood, a place full of fear where Dante stated there are three beasts – a leopard, a lion and a She-wolf standing in his way, preventing him from again waving that papyrus contract under the nose of a previously worried Michael Sullivan. He, the old man, was forever banned. Passing through the centre of gravity, Mr De-ville (Lucifer), as he was occasionally named, was never again to see the stars overhead.

# CHAPTER THIRTEEN

# "HATCHING, MATCHING AND CAREFULLY DISPATCHING"

'This Being of mine, whatever it really is, consists of a little flesh, a little breath and the part which governs.'

(Marcus Aurelius Antoninus)

On the twenty-second of March, 2014, I became, for the first time, a great granddaddy and I love it. Granddaughter Catherine, after being in labour too long and, after an uncomfortable and failed forceps delivery, she was finally prepared for the operating theatre; it was there where, after a Caesarean section was quickly performed, a perfect baby girl, weighing in at seven pounds, thirteen ounces, yelled her way into our world. The beautiful and much loved girl is named Beau. The first time I held her in my arms, I was so proud; a tear escaped from my eye, it falling down my cheek! During my Sunday radio broadcasts I often play a sung lullaby for baby Beau and along with new babies everywhere.

Prior to my travelling with the new granddad, west to Bangor Hospital, North Wales, and seeing the lovely new baby for the first time, before I knew what sort of delivery Catherine would undergo, a Doctor friend asked me if I should wish to be present at the birth. My eyes nearly popped out of my head! Horrified at the very thought, I declared: 'Not on your life, for that's "women's stuff where I wouldn't belong" and I'd rather run a mile than be involved!' Sexist or not, I would rather be one of those old fashioned men who pace up and down outside the labour ward until the miracle of birth is over and done with. Carl Sandburg stated: 'A baby is God's opinion that the world should go on.' He was obviously completely right.

Holding the wee child for the first time was a miraculous remembrance I wouldn't have traded for anything. It is so extraordinary, of holding which was inside, now on the outside; I don't think I'll ever get over the special moment. It will stay with me forever.

Motherhood has surely got to be the single hardest job in the world. You are forming people and you're giving them their values, and their morals, along with their expectations about life. It's like being a sculptor with a lump of unformed wet clay with only one chance to mould it into something spectacular. I don't envy young mothers and fathers today, that's for sure.

Children are not, of course, born civilised. They scream blue murder when they want something, piddle when they shouldn't, pour cereal over the clean floor and eat vegetables by the squashed fistful. They soon do horribly dangerously odd things which scare you half to death, yet we wouldn't swap any of them for the world. When Catherine needs a break from the broken nights, well this great granddaddy shall be there with the lullabies and Irish freedom songs – the only ones with sufficient verses which keep going all night long!

I wonder what the little one will become in adulthood? If Beau marries, I hope to goodness it will be a happy marriage. Que Sera Sera. Whatever will be, will be, I suppose.

A friend of mine once told me how there's no such thing as the perfect marriage, yet many are disillusioned only because they had unrealistic expectations in the first place. Do you know what it's like to look forward to a holiday for simply ages? Perhaps you fantasise, play music which is recognisable from the part of the world where you are travelling. You look forward to it so much. You plan to embark upon the things you have only read about in the guide books along with other literature concerning the destination. You have heard about the cafes and you are going to do a whole heap of this and that. Then the vacation arrives and everything goes very wrong. It's not the place you envisaged. To top it all, it pours with contant rain! Things which were supposed to happen, don't. You are deeply disappointed. It was more fun looking forward to the holiday, than the actual thing.

Well, that can be true of marriage. The looking forward part is sometimes, sadly, more fun than the actual event. It is amazing how many well known men and women had unhappy marriages. John Wesley and George Whitefield were not happily married men. Neither knew the joy of marital bliss. They were married, but it was a nightmare for each of them. Wesley's wife would come to hear her husband speak and then cackle during his sermon. Can you imagine how embarrassed he must have felt?

Madame Guyon, a seventeenth-century French mystic also had a miserable marriage; her biography is a heart breaking read. She did not marry the one she truly loved, but settled for second best, for someone else; she spent her life wondering what it must have been like to have married the one she really loved.

An unhappy marriage hardly needs refining. I am talking about when one is stuck, spending ones life with another, with someone you're not happy. It becomes a thorn in the flesh, which is painful. I know a close doctor friend who grew up and fantasised about being the perfect wife with that perfect husband. In her dreams she saw only bliss. She believed she'd enjoy companionship, affection, love, sharing and to grow old together gracefully. But no, it was anything but bliss. She watched others separate and she envied them. They divorced and she wished it could happen to her, yet she stuck it out until he died in 2008. Now alone, she wakes up every day, relaxing, emerging with a peace as a different person, never pointing the finger or becoming bitter, for, when all is said and done, it takes two to work at a see-saw, both working at it constantly and that's simply what I discovered with Maureen, my wife of over forty years. We both worked hard at a good marriage, doing our utmost to keep it good.

My very first love was naturally with my dear mother who was so ill, she regularly spitting fresh blood; as a patient she was in and out of hospital, suffering from pulmonary tuberculosis and, at only thirty-eight years of age, finally gave up the ghost, dying when I was only a little boy of almost four and, being such a very small child left behind, I had no chance of saying my goodbyes to her. Thirty-two years later, I was once more bitterly left behind; this time I was now grieving for my dear brother Paddy. It was a most dreadful, heart breaking loss.

Robert Browning declared:

> 'Grow old along with me!
> The best is yet to be,
> The last of life, for which the first was made.'

Even so, neither my beautiful mother nor my beloved brother were anything but old; they had no chance to grow old.

In this Western world of ours we do all in our power to withhold the ageing process, to stop ourselves from dying. We're encouraged by parts of the medical profession to keep ourselves fairly fit and nifty, doing away with the greying hair, to choose yet another shade or colour; we daily exfoliate our skin and invest in expensive moisturisers, one for the day and another for the night. When they all fail us, well, there's always either botox or the Harley Street surgeon, ready to offer, at a price, plastic surgery, unprofessionally known as the "nip and tuck"!

During the last World War both Vera Lynn, the forces' sweetheart and Gracie Fields sang:

> 'Now is the hour
> for me to say goodbye.
> Soon I'll be sailing
> far across the sea.
> While I'm away
> Oh, please remember me.'

It seems all too regularly for us to hear on the BBC 'News of some young soldier, sailor, airman, who'd died in Iraq, Afghanistan ... wherever, whatever, and we mutter: 'What a dreadful waste!' Death, we feel, should be for the elderly, the very old ... not someone so young, whereas a harsh ruler, such as Nicolae Ceausescu, the Romanian politician and dictator, saw his end after a brief trial. Much to the intense joy of the crowds in the Christmas of 1989, he, along with his wife Elena, was executed.

A man whose name I honestly do not know, was so distraught by the the abusive Brother Joe, the man who had harmed him, year in, year out in the Artane Industrial School hung around Dublin's Mater Hospital for days, waiting until he knew that Christian Brother was dead, never to abuse either him or anyone ever again.

We hold many reactions to the subject of death which really is a part of life and, if I dare so much as to mention my own immortality, a friend upbraids me, saying: 'Stop it, Martin, for I don't even ever want to hear you saying such a thing; right?' Whatever she or anyone else thinks, we shall all die one day; that's inevitable, yet, when it comes knocking on our door, we wish to run in all other directions rather than taking it head on; we begin stating how it just isn't fair.

And that's how I felt in the November of 2012, when Maureen, my wife, finally gave up the struggle with her invasive cancer ... that terrible cancer destroying her left lung. That is when I realised life was utterly unfair, totally unfair to me, to her much loved three kids, to those grandchildren.

From when I first met her back in the seventies, I knew I surely loved her. From the day we tied the knot here in Conwy, we became as happy as 'pigs in muck' – and I should like to add here how I acquired such an expression from my Jewish neighbour, so don't blame me! Tackle her – she can take it!

Maureen converted to Catholicism, simply so she could marry me in the Catholic Church ... to be married in a snow storm; the late Father Flanagan married us. She wasn't only a fine wife to me, but a good mother to her own offspring .

In the late 1980's Maureen had suffered a heart attack. Recovering well and attending a basic routine follow-up session with the Consultant Cardiologist, a chest X-ray displayed a highly worrying 'spot' in the left lung.

We hugged and did all the sort of things one tries to say and do in such a mind blowing situation. We made it our decision to include the three kids; when I say 'kids', well, they were all grown ups and I cannot quite remember who said what and when, but we were all totally supportive for her and of one another. It was recommended she travelled to England's Broadgreen Hospital, to see an eminent surgeon who alone was prepared to operate, drastically removing the entirety of my wife's lung.

With all the help and deep love from us all, her family, I swear there wasn't a single, solitary day which went by when we didn't help her and each other. We constantly remembered only those happier days, those days when we first encountered each other, during those times with the Llandudno Musical Players, when I was treading the boards, acting out my favourite musicals - hers, too.

I naturally miss Maureen so very much, yet I am told:

> There is a time for everything...
> a time to be born and a time to die,

...a time to weep and a time to laugh,
...a time to mourn and a time to dance,
...a time to embrace and a time to refrain,
...a time to keep and a time to throw away
...a time to love for he has made
everything beautiful; I know there is nothing
better for a man than to be happy and to do good
    while he lives.
I saw your tears, but I declare that the dead, who
    had already died are happier than the living,
    who are already alive.
                     (paraphrase on Ecclesiastes)

I personally wrote:

"I sit here alone with a tear in my eye,
Remembering of days of times long gone by
Of mountains, of valleys, of brooks and of streams,
Of the tall green grass, that held my sweet dreams,
The stone boat in Kimmage and the Sundrive
    Road,
All part of youth in sunshine and snow
From Dominic Street Orphanage where I shed a
    few tears,
Then on to Artane my school of dark years
Now all of the years that I spent in that school
We lived by the whistle and silence the rule;
The beatings were many, for the Brothers were
    cruel,
The leather, the cane, bend over that stool.

Twelve, three, eight, nine my number no name,
They took it from me as if I was to blame;
Twelve, three, eight, nine my number no name,
They took it from me as if I was to blame.

Now I left that old school at the age of sixteen,
Out into the world I had never seen;
From Dublin to Galway and places beyond,
Seeking a home where I might belong,
But I always remember the promise I made
When my son's in school you'll not hear him say:

Twelve, three, eight, nine my number no name,
They took it from me as if I was to blame;
Twelve, three, eight, nine my number no name,
They took it from me as if I was to blame.

Sometimes when alone I sit and dream,
But I know, when I turn, there'll be my Maureen;
She the light of my love, the love of my love
The lovely Maureen, oh, my lovely wife.

Twelve, three, eight, nine no number my name,
She shares it with me without any blame;
Twelve, three, eight, nine no number my name.
She shares it with me without any shame,
The lovely Maureen, oh, my lovely wife."

# CHAPTER FOURTEEN

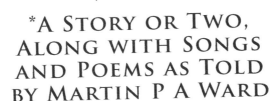

# *A STORY OR TWO, ALONG WITH SONGS AND POEMS AS TOLD BY MARTIN P A WARD

The Brightest Star:

The Victorian Mansion, with all its grandeur, was long gone, to have been replaced by some box like dwellings. Two of them were inhabited by a quiet pair, one being an artist, the other a kind pensioner, Charles Patrick James; to all and sundry he was known by his middle name, it shortened to 'Pat'. That was the way he liked it. That was how it was to be.

It was a bitterly icy cold day, yet, despite the depressing forecast, Pat needed to set off. He turned off his small radio; he'd been listening to it quite a lot, hoping to be gently entertained. He also checked his chicken and vegetable casserole, it slowly simmering in the Aga; hmm, it smelled good. Since his becoming a widower, sadly some five years previously, Pat became a dab hand at cooking for one. Once he returned home again, he would be more than prepared for a nice hot meal inside him.

Donning thick and hooded winter togs, he rediscovered his long fairisle knitted scarf, it given to him the previous year. He'd extracted it from the top drawer of his chest of drawers where he normally stored his socks and gloves. As he wound the length twice around his neck, Pat muttered to himself: 'That'll keep old Jack Frost at bay!'

At the request of his next door neighbour, his artist friend, Pat locked his front door. Reminiscing within himself, he remembered those long gone days when no-one bothered to lock up, never thinking of any perils. It seemed all so long ago, when folk felt safe in their beds.

The unadopted road, if one may name it a road, leading away from whence he came, he inwardly complained concerning the gravel path. In the summer months it threw up unwanted dust, with weeds growing high amidst patchy grass. Good on his feet, he approached the busy main road. Automatically, Pat turned into a leafy avenue where he bumped into two elderly sisters, Mabel and Cissy Cox. Rumours had it how Mabel was jilted at the altar; Cissy almost went off as a GI bride, yet that apparently came to nought.

'Good evening, Mr James. Are you off to the pond again?' asked the elder of the two.

Pat gave a nod.

'I see you're wearing the scarf I knitted for you,' added the other. 'It looks good on you.'

He half smiled, as if he'd remembered how he received it; he rarely struck up much of a conversation with either of those spinsters. 'Must be off now!' he declared. 'Things to do, eh?'

Pat passed by the newsagent's, the only bank and the unisex hairdresser's before approaching the grocery store, it directly next door to the pub where he sometimes enjoyed a quick game of pool. The latter two businesses were owned by fellow Irish folk – Mick and Molly Rand.

'Ah, there you are, Pat!' Molly exclaimed, handing him a large paper bag. 'Now, look ...there are all sorts inside.'

Pat peered to view chunks of soda breads, fruit buns and left over sponge cakes. 'All for my ducks, eh?' he asked.

'Of course,' she said.

'Well, they're not for you, old son,' Mick chuckled.

She ignored her husband's slight wit and continued: 'Don't you forget, Pat, how you're joining us for Christmas lunch tomorrow? All right?'

He offered his thanks. 'I could hardly forget that now, could I?' He was grateful not to be all alone upon such a special feast day. 'Now, you two, I must be on my way to the pond.'

Several years before, Pat, along with some willing locals, approached the parish council, as to whether it might be permitted to care for the village green, incorporating its own pond. The request became stamped: "accepted", upon the full understanding there were no major alterations to the conservation area.

Pat wondered what they meant by 'no major alterations'. Whatever, it was agreed, he adding to plant out various flower beds, some weeping willow trees, along with erecting a smallish fence surrounding a four feet green area for the dozen, or so, ducks, they being fenced in, to keep them all safe. In addition, there needed to be two small gates upon either side of the pond, to open up first thing in the morning and, obviously, close last thing at night, to lock up all the ducks.

A small grassy island, within the centre of the pond, was built. Mick and Molly raised some monies from their locals' tombola night, acquiring enough cash for this project, keeping the ducks free from feral cats and vixens, particularly at night. Pat enlisted a goodly number of willing helpers, yet, one by one, many soon found lame excuses to drop out, leaving only he and his chum, Larry Hogan, to keep up with the work.

Pat became personally responsible for checking the gates were locked on a Monday, Wednesday and Friday. In front of each gate were two long green benches, pleasant for all peoples to occasionally take the weight off their feet. He, too, invariably made good use of those seats, from where he'd feed the ducks, to where they'd all gather to consume their goodies. A good hearted man, Pat would often retain some of the buns, to ensure some of those old slow coaches consumed their fair share; he was anxious none went hungry. Once every last duck had waddled its way through the gate, Pat fastened it. Larry would hurry to lock the far side of the pond, ensuring every last Mallard was safe, he giving Pat the thumbs up.

It was about then an unusual sound caught Pat's attention; he glanced to see a frustrated young mother trying to cope with a lively puppy as well as pushing a baby-buggy in which was a well wrapped small infant. The baby, probably no more than nine or ten months, was mizzling. Tired, the woman asked Pat if she may, too, sit on the bench.

'Of course,' he said, moving up to make room for her. 'Your little one, though, doesn't sound too happy.'

Introducing herself as simply Annie, she explained how the baby, Beckie, short for Rebecca, was teething, hence the high redness in her cheeks. 'I thought the quacking from the ducks might distract her from the niggling pain.'

'Good idea,' agreed Pat. He stared down at the puppy, an attractive golden Labrador.'May I pick him up, Annie?'

She nodded, watching as the previously whimpering puppy nestled its head into Pat's lap, it peeping back at its owner, then up at Pat, as if to know everything was okay, okay, prior to falling asleep, all the time having its floppy ears massaged. 'Hush now,' Pat reassured the dog, yet the elderly man was more concerned to hear Beckie who was still grumpy.

He leaned forward. 'You won't understand a single word I am going to tell you, young Beckie, but, do you know what happens when a child cries?'

The little one looked up at him, seemingly to like the sound of his warm voice, to see the twinkles in his Irish blue eyes. Pat sensing this, he added: 'I'll tell you, Beckie. When a child cries, a star goes out in the sky, never again to be relit until the little one smiles again. Sometimes, when you gaze up at the sky, it's ablaze with miles and miles of smiles. Other times, when one stares up, there are only a few smiles. Shall we ask ourselves why, sweet one? Yes? Well, it's when you and your mammy look up, you'll see long streaks, rushing across the sky. Now, if you could talk, you'd probably ask some adults: "What are they?" You'd be told: "Comets, meteors, even falling stars!"

No, Beckie, they aren't any of those. They are the Star-lighters, all lighting up the stars of happily smiling children. Often, the night sky is all ablaze with stars, all from smiling faces; other times there are only a few. Why is that? It is because a bright star needs to actually come from a laughing child.'

Pat spoke on to tell the wee girl how it started all so many years ago, when a very new Star-lighter was instructed to choose the largest star, to make it into the brightest light, for the brightest smile, but, guess what he did? He grabbed hold of the most brilliant of stars and moved it right across the heavens. Wise men upon the eastern earth, saw that bright star moving across the night sky; they knew something awesome was taking place, hence, they decided to follow the particular star through days, weeks and even into months. Sleeping during the days, then following it at night, they journeyed on, wherever it went. After a long time, and nearing exhaustion, they came to the brow of a hill, to stare down into the valley below, halting, discovering where the star had stopped, it showing an unusually dazzling light below. Riding their lumbering camels, they three eastern men made their way down to where the very great light was blazing, it beckoning them into a cave. Inside were a whole host of animals, including cattle and lambs, they facing inwards where their breaths warmed the area. The foreigners who'd followed the brightest star, gently pushed their way through, discovering a new born baby, wrapped in swaddling clothes, his parents looking down at him with a great love. The baby smiled a very beautiful smile; outside, the brilliance of the star was still lighting up the night sky. The visitors all agreed how they were seeing something, someone greater than all mankind ... they were seeing the face of God. The wise men knelt before him, praying before leaving three special gifts, prior to their returning home via another route. All agreed they most definitely had seen the very brightest of stars and, above all, the most brightest of smiles the world had ever seen.

Therefore, either tonight or any other starry night your mother may take you out, she will point to the star which shall be yours, yours for now and all time, no matter where you go, whatever you do, that shall always be your star. No-one else may view your star … only you. The brighter your smile, the brighter your star!'

By then, Pat and Annie noticed Beckie's rosy cheeks had paled down to her normality; the uncomfortable teething pains had ceased.

Annie offered Pat a great thank you. 'You have been most kind for, finally, my baby girl is fast asleep,' she declared. 'Now, Pat, I have to be on my way. That puppy in your lap … well, we did buy him for Christmas, but we've recently rented an apartment where no pets are aloud.'

Pat stroked the puppy's ears. 'What are you going to do with him?' he quizzed.

'I was hoping my parents-in-law may adopt Josh – that's the name we'd given him -.'

'He is house-trained, I presume?'

She nodded.

Pat's brows knitted together as he thought for a moment or two. 'Well, you wouldn't let me have him, would you?' He told her how a dog would be company for him.

'Oh, of course!'

'Hmm. There's simply one condition, Annie …'

'What's that?'

'If you do want the puppy back, if your circumstances happen to change, I'll meet you back here on New Year's Day. If you're not here, then I'll know the dog is mine.'

Annie knew her situation wouldn't become any different. With her beloved Beckie, she walked off home.

Pat awoke the puppy from its dreaming snooze. 'It seems you're living with me now,' to which the dog wagged its tail. 'Let's go home now, pup.'

Reaching home, Pat fished out his door key, unlocking his front door and, before he could say: 'Jack Robinson' the dog was inside, warming himself by the Aga, smelling the delicious aroma from the chicken and vegetable casserole. Josh whined for some food.

'Hush now, hush now!' exclaimed Pat. 'Hush ...' He smiled, for it occurred to him, how the pup's new name needed to be: "Hush Now"!

* * *

Cold Nights:

> "It's too late for summer,
> it's too late for one;
> it's too late for loving.
> No warmth in the sun,
> winter is coming,
> bypassed the spring;
> my nights are cold
> now I have nothing.
> It's too late for summer.
> It's too late for one.
> It's too late for loving,
> no warmth in the sun.
>
> When I was young,
> my heart it was bright.
> Winters I cannot remember;
> all of my life was sunshine and fun;
> all of my life was laughter.
> Now that you've gone

199

and left me all alone
with nothing but a heart
wrapped in a cold, cold stone,
it's too late for summer.
It's too late for one:
It's too late for loving
now you have gone."

Strolling around Llandudno, the low clouds were becoming without shape and I was sensing a chilly change in the season. Too late for summer, the sweet smelling roses were well passed their best; gardeners were out dead-heading the sad blooms. August was giving way to the autumn months of September and October and, after the trees trembled away their red and gold leaves, the tourist town would soon become a cold, lifeless winter, wrapped in a cold, cold stone.

When I was a youngster, springs and early summers were magical times, occasions when we'd pick a buttercup and, placing it under our chin, we'd see if there was the shine of a brilliant yellow; if there was even the faintest of a glow, we should cry the fable: 'Oh, you must have a liking of butter!' Young girls would sit crossed legged upon the grass and, laughing together, make daisy-chained necklaces.

Now it was too late for summer, my summer?

✳ ✳ ✳

Retirement Day:

"Well, it's your retirement day
and you'll do whatever you may
with the clouds at you feet;
sure, you'll float down the street
on your retirement day!

200

It's yours, it's yours,
it's yours, it's yours,
it's your retirement day!
It's yours, it's yours,
it's yours, it's yours,
it's your retirement day!

You can hear your friends all say:
'It's your retirement day!'
With the clouds at your feet,
sure, you'll float down the street
on your retirement day!"

It was to become my sixty-fifth birthday on the twenty-third of February in 2004. Here, in the United Kingdom, women still officially become old age pensioners at the age of sixty years, drawing a sum of monies every week. For us men, at the time of writing this autobiography, it arrives five years later; now, upon reaching such an amazing milestone in my life, I naturally presumed it would also become my retirement day, for me to be no longer arriving for work at every shift. Not so. Just as I was planning all those golden years stretching out before me, I was approached by one of the more senior of the white collar management, requesting I remain within the firm's employ until the end of that same year. Even so, my yes to that extra time escalated until I was sixty-seven. Why? Oh, the management made it clear how I was a most valuable employee! Before long, he requested I should stay working until that year's ending. Not replying to him immediately, as was my want, I went home to give it some serious thought, to, of course, chat it over with my wife. I very soon returned to see my superior in his office and, rather than saying a firm no, I remained working until the twenty-eighth of December, 2006.

Months previously to my retirement a Scottish family removed from north of the borders and, coming to live nearby in Llandudno, the man in their household performed the self same job of work as I. As time went by, I chatted with those Scots as to how they celebrated New Year's Eve, which they knew as Hogmanay. The wife, the lady of the house, stated: 'We're having a Hogmanay party, Martin. Why don't you come and join us?'

I accepted her kind invitation and, as the clock struck midnight, we all sang Robert Burn's 'Auld Lang Syne'. Oh, I happily joined in with them on New Year's Eve, but it suddenly occurred to me how no-one had ever scribed a song about the landmark of the retirement day, a day for anyone approaching such a grand milestone. Some who retire may see it as a depressing time, as if they are being thrown on the scrapheaps of life, but I personally believe it should be a celebration time when we retire. Hence, I wrote the above appropriate verses; just as my Scottish friends were happy, laughing and joking on Hogmanay, so was I on my last day at work; I sang out to that happy tune, but from deep within my heart came the birth of my very own composition: 'Well, it's your retirement day!'

I had finally left work. All my life I'd worked and, throughout those adult years as a devoted family man, I was the bread winner, yet I jested how I'd never yet won a loaf of bread! As I sat in our living room, I puzzled; seized by a large bout of nostalgia, I inwardly questioned, having left my beautiful green Ireland, to where all the years had vanished. More to the point, what was rolling ahead of me, what and who lay before me?

The yesterdays in my youth is ever with me, stuck firmly in my memory; however, today brings hope, but all my tomorrows remain a mystery; it is still a unique experience for even the meteorologists. Do you understand what I am saying? I am quite sure you do.

\* \* \*

A Storm has broken:

> "Overnight a storm has broken, broken here in my heart;
> overnight a storm has broken, broken here deep inside.
> You are the cause, you are the cure.
> Listen to my heart and you'll know for sure,
> that a storm has truly broken, broken here in my heart.
> Hold my hand close in yours,
> take my heart; it's yours, for sure,
> then you'll know love has spoken, spoken here, deep inside.
> Overnight a love has broken, broken here in my heart.
> We are one, you and me, we, together, to the stars will fly;
> overnight, a love has spoken, spoken here in my heart."

Reading my above piece of work, it caused me to meditate upon the late American tenor Mario Lanza (1921-1959) when he sang out in 1988:

> "Be my love,
> for no-one else can end this yearning,

this need that you and you alone create;
Just fill my arms,
the way you've filled my dreams,
the dreams you inspire
with every sweet desire."

* * *

Let all the bells ring out!

"Let all the bells ring out; Christmas Day is near.
Can you hear the bells ring out, bringing Christmas
  cheer?
Ring-a-ling, ding-a-ling; listen to them chime!
Ring-a-ling, ding-a-ling; surely, it must be
  Christmas time.
Oh, how the bells ring out, bringing Christmas near.
Santa Claus brings his toys, for the girls and boys;
Santa Claus brings his toys, full of love and joy!
Oh, how the bells ring out, Christmas Day is here,
we can hear the bells ring out, full of Christmas
  cheer!
Ring-a-ling-a-ling; ding-a-ling-a-ling! Listen to
  them chime.
Ring-a-ling-a-ling; ding-a-ling-a-ling! Surely, it
  must be Christmas time?
Oh, how the bells ring out; Christmas Day is here!

Christ the Lord, born today in Bethlehem;
Christ the Lord, born today, for the good of all men,
let all the bells ring out, we can hear the bells
  ring out,
Christmas Day is here ...
Christ the Lord is born!"

204

Staying down in Brighton, I was in the employ of Alan West & Son, an electrical engineering firm. I was also lodging in some rather unsavoury digs, run by a young married couple with two children. I was none too happy with my lot. To top it all, it was a dark and cold Christmas Eve; I decided I would attend midnight Mass. I wrapped up well with a thick winter coat, a long scarf and woollen gloves. I had only been on the south coast of England for a few days and was unsure as to the whereabouts of the Catholic Church. As I walked along the wet streets, I turned a corner and heard some carol singing; it was then I spied a well lit church where a service was in full swing. I walked straight in through the church door and, genuflecting, nipped into one of the pews. It didn't seem all that different from the previous carol services in the past years. The congregation were just finishing 'In the bleak midwinter' and the choir master was announcing their next favourite: 'O, come, all ye faithful, joyful and triumphant!' which I knew very well, but only in Latin. I joined in, but my strong baritone voice virtually drowned all those songsters around me as I sang out in Latin:

> 'Adeste fideles Laeti triumphantes
> Venite, venite in Bethlehem
> Natum Videte regem angelorum
> venite adoremus
> venite adoremus
> venite adoremus Dominum.'

After the service finished, an elderly fellow stretched out a hand to welcome me, yet, with a slight grin, he informed me how I must be in the 'wrong' church;

WHEN IRON GATES YIELD TO FREEDOM

he told me it was indeed an Anglican Church and not a Catholic one.

'Ah, but how did you know I am a Catholic?' I asked.

He exclaimed: 'Well, here we don't sing 'O, come, all ye faithful' all in Latin!'

Whatever church we may attend, or not, Christmas, in my opinion, should be heralded in by a great gusto of fun, with everyone joining in, yet, please, not before the twentieth of December; right?

❋ ❋ ❋

The Golden Fiddle:

Sean and Colleen Duffy enjoyed the countryside – they had removed to their forty-seven acre farm generations before. Their kids, all adults now, had grown up amidst milking cows, a few suckling pigs, some free range laying hens, along with a noisy flock of geese which would rapidly see off any unwanted strangers.

The Duffys were basically good folk, leading modest lives, with a farm cottage full of mundane items like Wellington boots, buckets with scouring powder for cleaning, and invariably the smell of fresh baking wafting from Colleen's spick and span kitchen.

On a Saturday night Sean would kiss Colleen on her forehead and leave the draughty old farm cottage for one of his lively locals where he was like a national monument when it came to playing the fiddle.

'Where are you going, Sean?' his wife would ask with a regularity.

He'd shrug, for, making his way to the crossroads, if he turned left, he'd land up in Murphy's Tavern. Three quarters of a mile, straight on, Sean would show his face into Gallagher's pub. However, Sullivan's off to the right, could easily accommodate sixty to eighty Irishmen. Upon a warm summer's evening there'd be quite a crowd, they over spilling outside in their beer garden, too. At the end of Sullivan's long bar was a small bandstand, with musicians well able to view their entire audience, they all enjoying the Irish music.

Downing his favourite tipples of Guinness and Irish Whisky, Sean Duffy would beam a smile, declaring how he'd not be drinking the black stuff only for himself, but he would be saving others from becoming drunks, stating he was a man with high morals! One of the barmen chuckled, stating: 'It looks as if you're saving a lot of others from the demon drink, Sean!'

Sean nodded, but he was distracted, watching a man playing the boron drum.

He didn't know that particular drummer, but he knew well Seamus Doyle playing the Uilleann pipes. Seamus stopped for a short while to call up Sean, to plead with him to play the fiddle.

'When you play the fiddle, Sean, even the angels themselves sit upon the clouds of heaven, simply to listen to you!' called one of the regulars. 'Let's be hearing you play.'

Sean Duffy played and played until closing time. Having called time, the voluptuous landlady told him: 'It's well time you went off home now. Your Colleen will be wondering where you are.'

'Aye, but she's a good woman, to be sure.' Drunk as a Lord, Sean replaced his beautiful fiddle back in its bag and bade everyone a very 'goodnight'. He made his way back towards the crossroads, when the heavens opened. To prevent an Irish soaking, he clutched his bag, it containing his precious fiddle. Full of drink, he made a wobbly dash for a large spreading oak tree, to shelter under it from the pouring rain. In his confusion, he made his mistake, forgetting all around the base of that particular oak tree was the unique fairy-ring, a ring he'd crossed and broken; how dare he cross it without first begging permission? Whatever, as he lay there, Sean began to doze off. All at the self same time, he acquired the weird sensation of falling, as if he was being dragged down and down, way beneath the earth. Helpless as he was, he gave up, allowing himself to sleep so much more deeply until he awoke with a start, wondering where on earth he could be. Amazed, it seemed a place of brilliantly warm sunshine, with no harsh tarmac roads, just soft tracks.

Sean scratched his balding head, he seeing pretty little thatched cottages with white-washed walls and green doors. Each small and individual dwelling acquired a large orchard with ripe pears and red apples. All the front flower gardens had taken on a brighter hue caused by the admixture of another, discernible with reds, yellows, greens and blues.

'Glory!' Sean declared. 'This is all so lovely. I wish to goodness I knew where I was.' He also wished his Colleen could have some of those flowers; it was a while since he'd taken her some blooms.

'Sure, why would you want to know your whereabouts?' interrupted an odd voice. 'You have never been this way before.'

'I know, yet tell me where I am, please.'

'Okay. You, Mr Sean Duffy, are in the land of His Majesty, King Connor in the County of Galway.'

Sean wondered who, in the name of Mick's dad, was King Connor of Galway.

The strange voice seemed to read Sean Duffy's mind. 'Don't you know your Irish history ... your history of the Irish leprechauns?'

Sean was unsure.

'All right. Allow me to inform you,' the stranger continued on, teaching how there are thirty-two counties in Ireland, each with their own leprechaun king. 'Of course, there is the very highest king himself.'

'What? Who is ..?'

'The Ard-ri is the highest King, known as "King Connor McNessa".'

Sean had listened to all of this stuff, yet what was he doing in such a predicament? He wiped his hands across his head and peered down at his body, at all his clothes, for he was as tiny as all the leprechauns. 'What have you done to me?' Sean asked, wondering what his wife might have to say. 'Come on now – make me back to the size I normally am, If you don't ...'

'... and you'll do what?' grinned the little fellow.

Sean realized he was powerless upon to change. 'Why am I like this?' he questioned.

The leprechaun, who introduced himself as Flynn, declared: 'The King wants a word with you, to ask a big favour.'

'A favour from me?'

Flynn nodded.

'So, where is he then, eh?'

In the flash of an instance, the King himself was standing before Sean, he with a broad kingly smile upon his regal face; he wore a smart green jacket which didn't quite do up around his expanding middle. Upon his royal feet were huckaback shoes, all ready for dancing. Straightening his bejewelled golden crown, the

King tilted his head. 'I'll tell you, Sean, what the favour actually is,' King Connor McNessa began. 'Are you really ready to listen to me?'

Phew! He was all ears.

'My elder daughter is to be married tomorrow, and didn't our very best fiddler fracture his right wrist?' To cut a long story short, he tripped, putting his hand out to save himself. In so doing, he fractured his wrist; he now had his hand and arm in a plaster of Paris pot. 'He is obviously out of action for the next six weeks.'

'Why call on me? I am a small time farmer, not a bone doctor.'

'To be honest, Sean, there's no-one else who can play a fiddle like yourself. Listening ... well, there's many a night I've sat on the pub's roof, hearing you playing that instrument, playing with a touch as soft as butterfly's wings. When our man hurt his wrist, I simply knew it had to be you. You are the only one fine enough to play at my daughter's wedding,' He told Sean all he needed to do was to play during that wedding afternoon, followed by three days and two nights, before you may return home, to explain your absence to your wife, to all your kids, all grown up now.

Sean Duffy thought how he had no choice, yet, he told HRH, he'd be honoured. 'There's only one snag, your Majesty ...'

The King raised his eyes heavenwards. 'Now, what shall that be, Sean?'

'I only possess a full sized fiddle.'

With that, the King clicked his fingers and produced a small sized twenty-four carat gold fiddle and bow.

Sean's blue eyes widened. Immediately Sean tuned it, hearing how it sounded. The first few notes caused the entire village to come out, they trying to discover as to where the magical music was coming. As Sean stood to play, the locals tapped their feet to the beat, clapped and cheered; there was a true master of the fiddle for the wedding reception. Plying Sean with food and drink, he played on and on. The more beverage he consumed, the better he played and for three days and two nights, for the whole wedding. The little people danced and danced until they were panting for breath. The wedding of the King's daughter was a great success, beyond compare, and mostly down to Sean Duffy's ability.

The joyful honeymooning couple left for the Kingdom of Mayo.

The King couldn't thank Sean enough, yet he told him how it was time for him to return home. 'Just one thing more, Sean ...'

Sean Duffy sighed. 'What is it now, your Majesty?'

'When our younger child, the other Princess is to be married, my wife who is the Queen will obviously send you a wedding invitation!'

Sean smiled, giving a nod, before quizzing: 'How on earth am I going to return to my home?'

Sean began missing his wife's company and he was fairly sure his lady indoors would be as worried as to his whereabouts, too.

The kind old King stated how Sean Duffy should go into a very deep sleep and, when he awoke, all would be well for him once again. Sean gave a brief nod and settled himself down for a nice, comfy sleep, softly snoring until he awoke, large as life, still beneath the large old oak tree; he was feeling totally refreshed. There was no doubt he was not a little grubby from being under the oak tree, yet he was at least safe and well, his bag at his side, containing his fiddle. He stood and stretched, looking up at the sunny morning's skies. He felt lepping with hunger; he imagined a big Irish breakfast, complete with pork sausages and white pudding.

Making his way home to the farmhouse and, once inside, Colleen stared up at his unshaven chin. With tears, she questioned him: 'Where have you been, Sean, for we've searched high and low for you?' She added how all and sundry stated they hadn't seen him since he left the pub. 'Now, it's Tuesday … are you all right?'

Sean nodded.

'Thank God for that!'

'Ooh, Colleen, you won't believe where I've been … and, not a word of a lie, would I be telling you? You know, on Saturday night, as I reached the oak tree, the heaven's opened and I made a dash to shelter. Didn't I forget there was the fairy-ring all around it? I tramped straight through it, feeling myself being dragged way underground.' He explained on how, when he awoke, he was in the land of the leprechauns, with the King from Galway. 'He asked me to play the fiddle at his daughter's wedding.'

He told her the entire tale from thread to needle, watching her Irish eyes widening as he spoke.

'Oh, if you weren't such a good fiddler, I'd say you were a teller of tall tales. Anyway, it is good to have you home again. Would you like some breakfast? You must be hungry.'

'Hungry? I could eat a horse!'

As Sean picked up his bag, Colleen took it from him and made to place it upon the nearby dresser when, out from it, fell a small object. She stared at in in a shock type of amazement, hardly knowing quite what to say.

'Sean!' she exclaimed. 'What's this?'

He asked what was what. Reaching towards her, there to his surprise was a small gold case, about the size of a small jewel box. Surely, he hadn't bought her a ring? 'What's inside, Sean?' Colleen asked.

He shrugged.

The clasp was so tiny, she had to acquire a nail-file to prise it open. There was no ring, but instead, a small golden fiddle and bow. Sean and Colleen were both quiet for a long moment.

Sean plucked at the strings, causing the melodic, the sweetest sound ever to be heard.

'What did I tell you ... didn't I tell you I was down with the little people? Now, isn't that your proof?'

'Yes, Sean.'

'You believe me now?'

'I do.'

'You know what, Colleen?'

She waited for him to speak on.

'It's grand to be home, simply to see your smiling face. What shall we do with the golden fiddle?'

Next to his own full sized instrument, she rested the golden one. She looked up to hear him remind her how he was still hungry.

'I know, my man ... you could eat a horse!'

'Aye.'

## THE END

# Epilogue

To my dear readers,

There is a poem which states:

> *To every man there opens*
> *a high road and a low;*
> *and every man decides*
> *the way he shall go.*

What the verse states, I suppose, is that the choices of who we are, and what we become in our life, lies in our own hands, how it is continually reinvented in those two roads and we must choose one or the other. How fortunate many kids are today, yet, as a youngster, I literally had no choice. My formative years were chosen for me. Even my Christian names, given to me at my birth by my mother, registered and at my baptism when I was only a few weeks old, when the local parish priest poured holy water over my head, declaring: 'Martin Patrick Anthony, I baptise thee in the Name of the Father, the Son and the Holy Spirit ...' Even my names were replaced. Those sadistic Christian Brothers, when I was seven and a bit years, snatched them away and replaced them with the five digit number of Twelve thousand, three hundred and eighty-nine. I was forced to respond to both the numbers and a whistle.

I was a hurt and frightened young slave boy, no longer with names, only answering to those numbers and the shriek of the whistle, where silence was the rule!

Oh, there's been a whole heap I've shared through these chapters, not least my contentment, fearlessness, happiness, laughter and those secret tears I shed. I now know much about loving and being loved in return for a lifetime of the same.

Within these pages, I believe my life's gift is mainly through my tongue, telling stories and singing; my voice broke early, around twelve years of age, so with my baritone voice I'll happily sing for you. Simply speak up and ask me … go on and tell me your favourite song and I shall do my best to delight you, but only if I know it!

Herewith, I have named this book: 'When Iron Gates Yield to Freedom'. It seems a fitting title, for it came about one July evening. Janice Lockwood, knowing of my formative years, of my background, how I was incarcerated in Dublin's harsh and abusive Artane Industrial School and for almost nine long years, being shut in by high wrought iron gates. What was my crime, why was I there? I was in Artane simply because I was an orphan; my mother, at the age of thirty-eight, had died from pulmonary tuberculosis, when I was only four years of age. My daddy, in the Irish army, was an absentee father. Hence, there was literally no-one to care for me. Life, for me, began in a crummy orphanage prior to my transfer to Artane, where I was imprisoned behind those wretched gates. Not until I reached sixteen did those two gates open up, and open to my new found freedom.

Regards,
Martin P A Ward

# REFERENCES

*Artane Industrial School*
*Dublin, Ireland*

– Now recalled
   St David's School

*Catholic Boys' Home*
*previously run by*
*St Vincent de Paul*
*Dublin*

– Now derelict

*Dominic Street Orphanage*
*Dublin*

– It was closed
   and left derelict

*Downpatrick Road,*
*Crumlin, Dublin*

– Lizzie Ward
   resided there prior
   to her death

*Sundrive Road*
*Kimmage, Dublin*
*– the quarry is*
*now a beautiful*
*garden, + car park.*

Martin P A Ward
resided here from to
age of four years, prior
to going into Dominic Street
Orphanage.